TOURISM, BIODIVERSITY AND SUSTAINABLE DEVELOPMENT

TOURISM, BIODIVERSITY AND SUSTAINABLE DEVELOPMENT

(In 6 Volumes)

Market Research in Travel and Tourism

(Volume 2)

Editor

Prof. O.P. KANDARI
ASHISH CHANDRA

ISHA BOOKS
DELHI—110 033

Tourism, Biodiversity and Sustainable Development
(Tourism/Culture)

Rs. 5000 (Set in 6 Vols.)
Rs. 850 (Each Volume)

ISBN: 81-8205-033-2 (Set)
ISBN: 81-8205-035-9 (Vol. 2)

Published in 2004 in India by
Isha Books, D-43, Prithviraj Road
Adarsh Nagar, Delhi-110 033

Lasertypesetting by: Varsha Graphics, Delhi
Printed at: Chawla Offset Press, Delhi

Contents

Preface *vii*

1. **Nature of Travel and Tourism** **1**
Challenges for Tourism • International Airline Alliances • World Travel and Tourism Council (WTTC) • Sustainable Development and Travel and Tourism.

2. **Recent Developments in Travel and Tourism** **36**
Competition Issues in the Travel Trade • Competition Issues in Aviation • Towards an Integrated Approach • Economic Developments in Tourism • Economic Impacts • Environmental Impacts on Tourism • Socio-cultural Impacts on Tourism.

3. **Tourism Liberalisation** **127**
Sex Tourism • Trends in Tourism.

4. **Market Research in Travel and Tourism** **146**
Purpose of Tourism Statistics • International Visitors • Domestic Visitors • Factors of Tourism • Economic Importance of Tourism • Management of Cultual Changes • Impact of Globalisation •

Multicultural Identity • Influence of Culture on Economic Policy • Market Segments and Niches • Market Needs • Tourism Services Expertise • Strategies for Management.

5. **New Threats** 221
Benefit of Tourism • Domestic Tourism Expenditure • Segmentation of Tourism • Wine Tour Enthusiasts • Scenic Tour Seekers • Personal Explorers • Exotic Tour Seekers • Ocean Cruise Enthusiasts.

6. **Consequences of New Challenges** 258
Multiple Travel Markets • The Travel Industry.

Bibliography 297

Index 299

Preface

In an increasingly competitive world marketplace, being world class in all areas of business is a pre-condition for success. This doesn't just apply to winning customers in the international marketplace, the same rules apply to doing business in the domestic tourism and travel market. Traditional marketing methods are increasingly ineffective in the modern world whereby tourists have access to a wide array of information through the internet. What is vital is the creation of technology platforms that allow available products to be marketed in innovative ways by using the most up to date technology. Rather than spending vast amounts of money on traditional forms of marketing a much more effective use of public funds may be the encouragement and facilitation of the use of technology that will allow firms to help themselves. Co-operative marketing efforts by the private sector will be the way forward.

The generally low productivity of tourism-related industries compared to other sectors and the economy as a whole acts as a restraint on growth. Productivity is especially a problem in the core segments of tourism—hotels and catering. In these branches labour productivity is significantly below the average for the economy as a whole in industrialised nations. The small size and fragmented nature of many tourism enterprises inevitably means that the existing growth potential is not sufficiently exploited.

The question that arises is how to improve growth as measured in terms of value added per employee in the core sectors of tourism. This calls for an even greater utilisation of ICT to rationalise production and marketing of the chain of tourism services. Competition has created new conditions in the tourism world market that are leading to structural change. The benchmark in tourism in this context is the travel industry which has increased productivity with the help of economies of scale and scope.

In the travel trade, ICT has substantially reduced the cost of managing organisational processes, despite rates of production, which are rapidly increasing. The networking idea has been especially attractive as a means by which small and medium sized firms can collaborate to compete more effectively in the global marketplace. The premise is that clustering and networking among smaller firms provides them with the potential to achieve collectively more than they could individually, in accessing and competing in world markets.

Editor

1

Nature of Travel and Tourism

Unlike many industry sectors, tourism is unable to be defined simply as a group of businesses that produce particular, similar products. Rather, the 'tourism industry' embraces a diverse range of providers and users of a variety of goods and services, and overlaps with other sectors of the economy.

However, the elements of tourism may be described in the conventional terms of 'supply' and 'demand'. 'Supply' involves the companies which deliver tourism products and services, including tour operators and travel agents, and companies for which tourism is not the main focus of business, but a component, such as accommodation, restaurants and cafes.

The performance of the supply side of tourism can be measured in terms of a variety of indicators, including employment, profitability, investment and company formation growth rates. Tourism 'demand' is usually measured in terms of the number of tourists, the number of nights they stay in hotels or other types of accommodation and the money they spend.

Tourism demand can be divided into groups by purpose of visit, such as people taking holidays, people on business travel, and people visiting friends and relatives. Tourism is becoming an important part of many regional communities as traditional industries decline. The development of tourism opportunities is important not only in the increased spending patterns in regional areas, but the flow on effects such as the development and maintenance of transport, communications and training infrastructure.

Tourism is not defined separately as an industry in the Australian and New Zealand Standard Industrial Classification (ANZSIC). To overcome this, the Australian Bureau of Statistics has developed a concept of 'tourism related' industries. Tourism-related industries produce products that are strongly associated with tourism and are classified into 'tourism characteristic' industries and 'tourism connected' industries.

Tourism-characteristic industries are: travel agency and tour operator services, taxi transport, air and water transport, motor vehicle hiring, accommodation, and cafes, restaurant and takeaway food outlets. Tourism connected industries include clubs and pubs, food manufacturing, automotive fuel retailing, casinos and other gambling services, libraries, museums and arts, and education.

A number of significant tourism sectors such as attractions and meetings and incentives, conventions and exhibitions do not neatly fall into the above definitions but consume products from a number of tourism related industries. Many other businesses may derive a smaller, but nonetheless significant, component of their returns from visitors or visitor activities.

Around the world, tourism has expanded dramatically over the past 30 years, and it looks set to continue growing. The services industry, of which tourism is an important part, is currently the main driver for growth among countries in the Organisation for Economic Cooperation and Development (OECD). International trade in services is currently around 20 per cent of total OECD trade.

Tourism represents 30 per cent of that international trade in services in OECD member countries. In terms of revenue, OECD countries generate about 70 per cent of world tourism activity. Tourism is an increasingly competitive industry internationally, with a number of nations, including New Zealand and the United Kingdom, actively pursuing tourism industry development strategies.

In addition, the downturn in the international market resulting from the events of September 11 last year has prompted the main tourism destination nations, for example, Canada, to increase their international tourism marketing efforts and to focus on visitor safety.

The World Tourism Organisation (WTO) is a well regarded international body that monitors trends and identifies areas for growth in international tourism. European countries receive the largest number of international visitors, for example, France currently receives around 75 million visitors per year. In this respect, Australia ranks twentieth out of OECD countries.

The higher ranking countries all have access to short haul markets that do not rely on air transport, while Australia relies on air transport from both its long and short haul markets, such as the United States, Malaysia and New Zealand. The World Tourism Organisation defines long haul travel as all travel except intraregional travel. Regions are Africa, Americas, East Asia/Pacific, Europe, Middle East, and South Asia.

Short haul travel, therefore, is intraregional travel. For example, Thailand or Japan would be regarded as short haul markets for Australia according to this definition. Clearly, Australia does not fit easily into this definition, as trips from many Asian countries require a considerable number of hours in the air, which is likely to affect traveller choice in destination. Tokyo-Sydney, for instance, takes around 10 hours, whereas Tokyo-Seoul takes around an hour.

International visitor numbers to East Asia have the highest growth rate, (14.3 per cent in 1999-2000), with Malaysia, China and Vietnam the strongest performers.This is in part due to an overall economic recovery in this region following the Asian economic crisis of 1997.This also partly reflects improved accessibility by air, with more flights serving more destinations and more airports increasing their capacities.

Australia is a long haul destination for traditional source markets including the United States, Canada, the UK, Germany and Europe. Australia's capacity to attract long haul traffic is reflected in its market share, which currently sits at around 0.7 per cent of total global international arrivals. The expected 10.4 million visitors by 2012 will increase Australia's market share to over 0.9 per cent. This is primarily because the forecast growth rate in Australian international arrivals is higher, at an average of 7.3 per cent annually over the next ten years, than the world growth rate forecast of 4.2 per cent over a similar period.

Longer average lengths of stay in Australia are recorded from Continental Europe and Canada, whereas shorter average lengths of stay are recorded from Japan, New Zealand and Singapore. China records a longer average length of stay for a number of market segments, including students. Generally, the further a market is away from Australia, the greater the visitor expenditure, over a longer period of time, yielding a higher average expenditure per person.

This partly accounts for Australia's capacity to capture a higher proportion of world tourism revenue of between one and two per cent.Number of overnight visitors Figure 1.2 shows that Australia's ranking rises to tenth among OECD countries in terms of the number of overnight stays in hotels and similar accommodation.

The higher ranking reflects the propensity of visitors to Australia to stay longer. While Australia attracts a small proportion of the total number of tourists worldwide, the industry's importance to the Australian economy is significant. Inbound and domestic tourism combine to become a major contributor to Australia's national and regional economies.

Until recently, hard data on tourism's economic performance was difficult to find. While good data is available on the supply of, and demand for, various tourism related goods and services, the National Accounts-which provide the official measure of industries' contributions to the Australian economy-do not include a measure of tourism's contribution.

This is because tourism does not fit the usual supply oriented definition of an 'industry': that is, a group of businesses that produce similar products. Rather, tourism can be defined only by reference to the demand for tourism products and services. To address this problem, the Australian Bureau of Statistics launched the Australian Tourism Satellite Account in October 2000.

The Satellite Account figures for the year 2000-2001 show that the tourism sector directly contributed 4.7 per cent-or $31.8 billion-to gross domestic product (GDP). In 2000-01, the tourism sector contributed 11.2 per cent of Australia's total export earnings, making it the fourth largest contributor-after mining, manufacturing and agriculture-and the largest export earner within the services sector.

Total tourism consumption in the year 2000-01 was $71.2 billion, an increase of $13 billion from 1997-98. Of that, 76 per cent ($54.1 billion) was consumed by domestic visitors and 24 per cent ($17.1 billion) by international visitors.

During 2000-01, the sector directly employed 551 000 people, or 6 per cent of all people employed in Australia. This is an increase of 35 000 people from 1997-98. Furthermore, according to Bureau of Tourism Research estimates, the sector indirectly employed an additional 340 600 people (in 1997-98), or another 4 per cent of those employed.

The tourism industry predominantly consists of small businesses. Over 88 per cent of businesses in the accommodation, cafes and restaurants sector and over 96 per cent of businesses in the cultural and recreational services industry are small businesses, employing less than 20 employees. In addition, there is a large number of non- employing, owner-operated businesses in the accommodation, cafes and restaurants sector.

Business formation and exit rates can be an indicator of growth and demonstrate changes in the structure of the industry. The availability of this information, particularly for business formation, is scant and for the tourism industry the problem is exacerbated by the difficulties in defining what businesses should be included in tourism data collections.

Challenges for tourism

Australian tourism is facing constant challenges, especially following the events of September 11 last year and the collapse of Ansett in the domestic airline industry. While some areas of tourism are still experiencing difficulties in the marketplace, the industry can look forward to strong opportunities for growth over the medium to longer term, stimulating new investments and creating new job opportunities, especially in regional Australia.

In environmentally sensitive areas, tourism can also help neutralise land and resource use conflict by offering sustainable alternatives. To fully realise tourism's potential, as a driver of economic growth and as an environmentally sustainable industry, requires a strategic plan-both to capture opportunities and to deal with challenges.

This is particularly so in light of the expected doubling of international visitor numbers, along with a significant increase in domestic tourism, over the next decade. Many overseas tourism destinations cope with far higher tourist flows than Australia. However, the impact of an additional five million visitors per annum to Australia, together with the growth in domestic tourism, will affect the whole tourism industry as well as regional communities dependent on tourism.

It will also expose pressure points, in terms of both the adequacy of tourism infrastructure and the ability of particular destinations to sustainably cope with extra visitors and still offer a high quality tourism experience. However, tourism growth will not occur unless Australia makes the necessary investments in tourism product and related infrastructure to meet demand.

The tourism industry's ability to attract new investment has been hampered by perceptions of low profitability in the sector and the cyclical nature of the industry. This new infrastructure is adequate to meet the expected demand and, if not, how investment in tourism infrastructure and product can be boosted. How to enhance the image of the tourism industry with investors is another key area for consideration.

Almost all visitors to Australia arrive by air. This raises issues about the adequacy of airline capacity and airport infrastructure. One suggestion is the establishment of a 'northern hub' in Cairns for international services. This could help to disperse international visitors and provide wider international access to existing and new tourism products in regional Australia.

Similarly the capacity of immigration procedures to respond to an increased flow of visitors, while maintaining border integrity, will be important, particularly in an environment of heightened security procedures.

The adequacy of Australia's current transport modes to disperse tourists around the country is fundamental to the spreading of the potential economic benefits associated with tourism. This raises questions about the planning and funding of new rail routes and road infrastructure in both urban and regional Australia.

With competing demands for scarce public resources, governments are increasingly moving towards developing partnerships with the private sector to fund and operate road and rail infrastructure. The issue of developing a system of grading for tourism infrastructure, which may assist in setting priorities for infrastructure investment.

The tourism industry needs skilled, innovative staff and managers. Some commentators believe that there are already shortages in skilled personnel in certain categories. Unless these are addressed, the standard of tourism products being offered may not satisfy customers and potential tourism growth may be impeded.

Domestic tourism constitutes more than 75 per cent of visitor nights and visitor expenditure in Australia. A small increase in domestic tourism can, therefore, significantly boost revenue for tourism operators. Domestic tourism is growing at a slower rate than the economy as a whole and at a significantly slower rate than inbound tourism. This raises questions concerning appropriate drivers of demand for domestic tourism and how these can be influenced. Impacts on the natural environment and in communities also need to be considered.

Recent global events have had a significant impact on tourism. Australia is vying for international tourists in an increasingly competitive global market. This raises questions about access to inbound markets, pricing and distribution strategies, and the availability and the quality of tourism products. The image of Australia in international markets is also important.

Since 1985, the number of French tourists to the U.S. has tripled, reaching more than one million in 2000. France ranks third among European markets, after the United Kingdom and Germany, and sixth in the world after Canada, Mexico, Japan, the U.K., and Germany as an overseas source of income for the tourism industry in the U. S.

It is clear that September 11 had a major impact on the French travel & tourism industry, particularly on those who were promoting travel to the United Sates. Nevertheless, travel to the United States had already experienced a decline in outbound travel to the U.S. over their 2000 figures prior to September 11.

Although there have been some recent signs of a mild recovery, France's "Visit USA" industry continues to suffer from the consequences of those tragic events. The Commercial Service of the Department of Commerce is actively promoting U.S. tourism destinations and considers it one of its "best prospect" sectors.

The Visit USA Committee France, a private industry association aimed at promoting the United States as a travel and tourism destination, is the most prominent and active organization in France promoting tourism to the United States. Today, the Visit USA Committee/ France has more than 100 members, including 22 U.S. states and 20 cities, as well as major U.S. airlines, hotel chains, car rental & services companies, theme parks, and tour operators.

A report by the World Travel & Tourism Council shows the European Union as the largest regional generator of travel and tourism in the world, followed by the combined U.S./Canadian market.

International arrivals to the U.S. are forecast to grow for the next three years by more than 4 percent per year. Europe will continue to be the top tourism generating overseas region with visitor arrivals expected to surpass 13 million by 2004, a 19 percent increase over 2000. Asia will grow fastest as a region, and is forecast to reach 9.3 million visitors by 2004, a 23 percent increase over 2000.

Visitors from South America will reach 3.6 million, a 22 percent increase over 2000. International arrivals to the U.S. are forecast to decline in 2001, but will begin to recover in 2002, and then grow by over 7 percent per year through 2004. Europe will continue to be the top tourism generating overseas region, but visitor arrivals will be down substantially in 2001 (-21%). Arrivals are forecast to return nearly to 2000 levels by 2004.

Asian arrivals will decline in 2001 (-19.8%), but return nearly to 2000 levels (7.5 million arrivals) by 2005. France will continue to be among the top tourism generating overseas country, but visitor arrivals will be down substantially in 2001 (-14%). Actually, arrivals from France are a two-part story in 2001. For the first half of the year, the U.S. as a destination registered significant growth from France.

For the second half of the year, the United Kingdom, Germany, France, Italy, Spain, Sweden, and Switzerland all showed declines in arrivals. Among the top three markets in Europe, annual declines were seen in Germany (-17%), France (-14%), and United Kingdom (-4%).

The U.S. is a popular destination, ranked number one among long-haul destinations, just behind the French

West Indies. French visitors are very attracted by the sea, beaches and sun. This explains the popularity of destinations such as Florida and California. As the French are also highly fond of culture and history, many French visitors choose cities renowned for their artwork or museums.

In addition, images of cowboys and Indians, and open spaces, fostered by American TV shows and movies, remain vivid in the French imagination, which explains why Western states are also popular in France. New York, Florida, California, the national parks in Arizona, Nevada, and Utah remain the top choices as destinations for French travelers. New York is the major gateway.

Florida offers the sun, beaches and amusement parks. California offers sun, projects an appealing lifestyle, and is an entry point to many national park areas. The travel arrangements are offered in all tour operators' brochures through: city-package plans, with an average length of stay of 5 to 7 days. Only 25 percent of these plans offer only the beach and sun; 75 percent offer city stays including sightseeing and airport transportation, mainly in New York, Washington D.C., Boston, Chicago, Los Angeles, San Francisco, New Orleans, Las Vegas, Miami, and Orlando.

Most importantly, the French customer is a repeat visitor who, having experienced the most popular destinations, is now looking for new activities and destinations. In the South and in the West in particular, Texas, New Mexico, Wyoming, Montana and Colorado, are attracting more and more French visitors looking for outdoor activities and sports (hiking, golfing, surfing, skiing).

New England, Washington, D.C., Louisiana, and other parts of the south (such as Missouri, Georgia, North Carolina and South Carolina), are also becoming more popular. For the past few years, states in these regions have launched significant promotional campaigns in France.

The French have 5 weeks of statutory paid vacation each year. Tourism in France is seasonal: one week is generally taken in winter (February), one week in spring (April), and three weeks in the summer (between June 30 and September 15), traditionally during school vacations. The fact that the French all leave at the same time is a major concern for the airlines, which are oversold at such periods and below capacity during the rest of the year.

The growth of French travellers has been affected by the September 11 tragic events. As a consequence, French travellers have shortened their length of stay in the United States by a few days. To reduce the effects of what has been until recently a strong U.S. dollar, some French tour operators have offered discounted packages. In the same spirit, a few New York City hotels have significantly cut their room rates to remain attractive to the French market.

The strengthening of the Euro vis-a-vis the dollar in recent months should help to regenerate travel to the United States in the months ahead and may counteract some of the lingering effects of September 11. Numerous American tourism professionals view France as a challenging market.

However, marketing strategies that are adapted to the French market's specific characteristics can help committed destinations to overcome these challenges.

The objective of any marketing strategy should be to reach the end-user as directly as possible. The public can be reached through press coverage (press familiarization trips), the Internet, and all forms of advertising.

Promotion through the press is the most reliable advertising tool, keeping in mind that press releases and promotional materials should preferably be in French. Media have a great impact in France and should be considered as an excellent means to promote tourism to the United States. Travel trade shows, such as Top Resa, are also extremely attractive and effective vehicles to promote new and undiscovered U.S. destinations.

International Airline Alliances

The airline industry is now in a highly competitive environment, as most carriers are going through structural changes and mergers and acquisitions in order to compete in an ever-changing marketplace. For example, airlines are beginning to introduce ticketless travel, which will affect travel agent commissions.

Currently, most airlines are offering ticketless travel on international flights. These factors will have an impact on tour operator and travel agency programs. Also, by cooperating with their American and other competitors, European airlines can now offer their customers more destinations and services. Examples of cooperation includes: frequent flyer mile reciprocity, simplification of ticketing, better flight connections, harmonization of tariffs and services, and code sharing.

Nevertheless, the shortage of flights to the United States has become a major impediment to renewed growth in travel to the U.S. There are now five major international airline alliances. Stare alliance, created in 1997, this alliance includes Air Canada, Air New Zealand, All Nippon Airways, Austrian Airlines Group (Austrian Airlines, Lauda Air and Tyrolean Airways), Ansett Australia, British Midland, Lufthansa German Airlines, Mexicana Airlines, Scandinavian Airlines (SAS), Singapore Airlines, Thai Airways International, United Airlines and Varig Brazilian Airlines.

Lost-cost airline companies began to be created after the Gulf War (1991) to compete against airlines located in the western part of the U.S. The pioneer was Shuttle by United, followed by Southwest Airlines, founded in 1974 in Dallas. With a possible potential of 15 percent of the world market, the low-cost companies now represent 5 percent world airline traffic.

In 1999, Air France, the French flag carrier, was partially privatized and was looking for new alliances in order to compete against its main European rivals, British Airways and Lufthansa. The French Government still holds a stake in half the company. On June 22, 1999, Air France and Delta Air Lines announced the creation of a new partnership, thus creating the latest global airline alliance.

The partnership represents 149 million passengers, 800 airplanes, 365 destinations. The partnership with Delta would create $ 157 million in extra revenue each year and result in substantial cost savings. Together they control one-fifth of the transatlantic market. In 2001, Air France ranked first among French carriers with 40.1 million passengers, an increase of 17.7 percent over 2000, compared to Air Liberté, with 4.4 million passengers, and AOM, with 3,35 million passengers.

On November 7, 2001, Air France re-establish its direct Paris/New York Concorde daily flight, following a hiatus caused by the July 2000 crash at Charles de Gaulle airport. In addition, British Airways will open two daily flights. Importantly, Roissy/Charles de Gaulle (CDG) airport is Air France's hub. CDG airport is Europe's third leading airport (in terms of passenger numbers) after London Heathrow and Frankfurt.

On March 2002, Air France launched an advertising campaign in order to counteract the decrease in international traffic. For example, the company is offering a special package at 350 Euros to seven major cities in the U.S. The United States and France signed a bilateral air service agreement on October 20, 2001, pursuant to an initial agreement concluded in April 1998. This "open skies" agreement entered into effect in the first quarter of 2002. Its four-year period of implementation includes authorization for a 40 percent increase in services by U.S. airlines to France with an equal number authorized by French carriers to the U.S.

After four years, air service between the U.S. and France will again be open for renegotiation. The new agreement will allow French and American carriers to serve any airport and to establish code-sharing partnerships. It should also lower air fares by boosting competition. This agreement enlarges the services between the U.S. and France that have been in effect since 1998.

United States-France air traffic has increased by 180 percent over the last decade, reaching 6.4 million passengers in 2000, allowing French airline companies in particular to increase their market share-from 30 percent in 1993 to 47 percent in 2000. After the September 11 tragic events, some U.S. carriers have decided to suspend some of their daily flights.

The average French person visiting the U.S. is between 25 and 45 years old. The average length of stay is approximately 12-16 days. Daily French visitor spending in the U.S. amounts to approximately $ 100. The French travel customer is becoming increasingly demanding, searching for "tourism products" in such areas as culture, health, and adventure. The need to respond to this demand is reflected in the catalogues of major tour operators that now have to find new promotional tools to attract customers. In addition, such customers require a great deal of specialized service.

Nevertheless, a category of tourists, mainly retired people, prefer organized trips. A potentially effective strategy for promoting U.S. destinations in France is to promote American uniqueness while recognizing that the French have a keen interest in history and historic places. A recent survey published by the national association of French travel agencies shows that 70 percent of French people visiting the U.S. will visit historic sites and national parks. The French are also looking for personal interaction with the local population.

French travelers are becoming increasingly adventuresome and are willing to try different experiences. At the same time, most French travelers like good food, including French cuisine. The French are also attracted to ethnic foods, which are available increasingly in France itself. In the United States, French travelers especially appreciate natural and scenic sights; national parks; shopping; driving what they call "une belle américaine" (a big American car) on freeways; jazz music; American breakfasts; McDonald's; popcorn; hot-dogs; the Hard Rock Café; and theme parks.

French tour operators have adapted themselves to the needs of the market and concentrated on products offering plenty of opportunities to explore and satisfy individual interests. Most of the tour operators are now selling directly to the public. In recent years, the tourism industry in France has experienced a series of mergers and acquisitions, which will have an important impact on the structure of the tourism promotion industry in France.

After the September 11 attack, in France, twenty tour operators registered 11,000 cancellations for trips to the United States and Canada during the days that followed the attacks, and nearly 5,500 reservations were cancelled in October for those destinations. Sales also dropped for Mediterranean destinations. Although there was an overall downturn immediately after September 11, travel rebounded significantly several months later. Travel to the United States and the Middle East (Syria, Jordan, Israel, Egypt), however, remains slow. Other destinations are now emerging as leading destinations, such as Malta, Portugal, Thailand, Mauritius, the Seychelles Islands and the Maldives.

Some travel and tourism players in France have privately urged the United States government to take additional steps to help promote travel to and tourism in the United States. These top European Tour operators now hold nearly 70 percent of the market and represent a turnover of $ 39,5 billion. In 2001, takeovers and mergers have increased, mainly because French tour operators are too small and too specialized and cannot survive.

There are approximately 6,000 travel agencies in France. Independent travel agencies are usually members of associations. In 2001, e-tourism represented a turnover of 892 millions Euros. E-tourism has experienced significant growth in the past two years, with a significant increase in the number of such firms. Tour operators online are competing in the e-travel business. A notable trend has been for tour operators to develop agreements with e-portals.

There are 27 million e-travelers in Europe. France represents 2.5 million e-travelers. The Internet is used by 17-25 percent of French e-travelers to obtain information about trips. However, only 5 percent have actually bought a package on the Internet.

World Travel and Tourism Council (WTTC)

The World Travel and Tourism Council (WTTC) is the forum for global business leaders comprising the presidents, chairs and CEOs of 100 of the world's foremost travel and tourism companies. Since 1990,WTTC has been raising awareness of the contribution that Travel & Tourism makes to the whole economy, demonstrating a far greater impact than had previously been realized.

Over the same period, a shift has taken place in the consciousness of the western world. There is a growing concern about poverty and the widening gap between rich and poor, with evidence of a return to community principles. In the private sector, while profit is the foundation on which business is constructed, many companies are now seeking ways to create value for society while creating value for their business.

In the past 50 years, globalization has helped to generate unprecedented prosperity. At the same time, the world faces enormous and critical challenges. Persistent poverty in many areas, mismanaged economic development, environmental degradation, social inequalities and disappearing cultural heritage all threaten to undermine the progress that has been made.

There has been a growing emphasis by world leaders on the need for long-term 'sustainable development' - pursuing needed economic growth in the present, while preserving the natural and human environment on which quality of life and future growth depend. This has been the subject of two successive world summits: the 1992 Earth Summit in Rio de Janeiro and the 2002 World Summit on Sustainable Development in Johannesburg, South Africa.

Many companies have a long tradition of corporate philanthropy, taking a portion of their profits and returning it to society as charitable contributions to a variety of causes. However, with the emergence in the last decade of a global market-based economy, there is a growing consensus that the private sector has a larger role to play.

It is recognized that companies have social responsibilities that go well beyond their commercial duties and the traditional role of wealth generation and profit making. There is increasing interest in their capacity to help mitigate the negative aspects of globalization and proactively address issues facing society. The new standard is for business to exercise 'corporate social responsibility' (CSR).

While there is no single definition of CSR, it clearly does not refer just to charitable contributions detached from a company's core business. It means adopting open and transparent business practices that are based on ethical values. It means responsibly managing all aspects of operations for their impact not just on shareholders, but also on employees, communities and the environment.

Ultimately, CSR is about delivering sustainable value to society at large, as well as to shareholders, for the long-term benefit of both. There is evidence that various 'stakeholders' in the global market - business, consumers, investors, employees, governments and local communities - are beginning to make choices that reflect this new standard: polls indicate that some consumers are making product choices based in part on the producer's ethical reputation.

In the private sector, many businesses, including the majority of FTSE 100 companies in the UK, now include social and environmental commitments in their core mission statements. A growing number are also adopting 'triple bottom line reporting' in which social and environmental results are measured and reported next to financial results.

However, these developments are not yet happening at a sufficient pace to create an effective force for change. Recognizing this, some visionary business leaders at the forefront of this trend are personally, as well as professionally, committed to making a difference and demonstrating social leadership.

Corporate social leadership means going beyond managing a company's impact, to actively seeking ways that companies can leverage their grassroots presence and unique capabilities to help tackle social problems. According to Steve Hilton and Giles Gibbons in their book, Good Business, it means finding a dual purpose, social as well as commercial, for every aspect of company operations. This approach requires vision by senior management, demanding a long-term commitment to build an intangible asset that may not have immediate financial returns, and a willingness to make changes to the company's management structures.

These visionary business leaders - who make the creation of value for society an integral part of creating value for their companies have the opportunity to be part of the solution to challenges facing the world, benefiting both business and society.

Because of its size and its interconnectedness with all parts of the economy, Travel & Tourism is one of the largest sources of economic activity in the world. At the same time, it can be an important force for sustainability by raising living standards in underdeveloped areas, promoting preservation of the natural and human environment and providing a vehicle for peaceful international exchange.

Travel & Tourism can be part of the solution to the world's challenges because of these key characteristics, which are described further below:

— As one of the world's largest and fastest growing industries, Travel & Tourism is, and will continue to be, a significant source of growth and prosperity worldwide.

— Using Tourism Satellite Accounting, an accredited econometric tool, WTTC each year measures the full economic impact of Travel & Tourism in over 160 national economies. The results have shown that this impact is far greater than had previously been expected. According to WTTC research, Travel & Tourism generates economic activity worldwide representing over ten per cent of total global GDP. The industry also accounts for over 200 million jobs (direct and indirect).

— With 4.5 per cent growth forecast per annum for the next ten years, Travel & Tourism is not only one of the world's largest, but one of its fastest growing industries.

— Travel & Tourism can help raise living standards and alleviate poverty in underdeveloped areas.

Present in local communities throughout the globe, Travel & Tourism is often an early investor and one of the few sources of economic activity in some of the world's least developed areas. As a consequence, it can raise incomes and contribute to poverty alleviation by:

— Stimulating the development of infrastructure that underpins the entire economy, including: transport such as airports, seaports and roads, public utilities to supply water and power and recreational facilities such as parks, stadiums and museums.

— Generating demand for a wide variety of locally supplied goods and services, providing jobs and training for local people and opportunities for entrepreneurs;

— Employing women, youth, the unskilled and people in rural and remote areas, who might otherwise have few opportunities.

— Travel & Tourism is regarded as the best development option in many emerging economies, an effective way of utilizing their natural and cultural resources to create jobs and wealth. The share of international tourism arrivals to developing countries grew from 19 per cent in 1980 to 30 per cent in 2000.

— Travel & Tourism provides powerful market incentives to protect and preserve fragile ecosystems, endangered wildlife and unique cultural heritage.

— Travel & Tourism's 'product' is the places that people visit. Protecting destination communities - the people, their unique cultures and beautiful natural settings - is critical.

Failure to maintain their well-being destroys the very attractions on which the industry depends directly for success. Unfortunately, this lesson has often been learned the hard way, after damage to local environments, for example, or after a decline in local community conditions has led to a reduction in tourism.

For governments, tourism can represent an alternative 'use' for natural and cultural resources that might otherwise be destroyed - by land development, by illegal activities such as wildlife poaching and the looting of ancient cultural sites, or through neglect. Tourism often provides a better economic return on these valuable assets, while rewarding their long-term preservation.

As a primary medium of international exchange, Travel & Tourism brings people from diverse cultures together. In a very real way, Travel & Tourism depends on international peace and prosperity. By creating opportunities for hosts and visitors to learn about each other and share experiences, tourism can even contribute to international understanding and term, has the potential to build bridges of peace.

For all these reasons, the Travel & Tourism industry has a vital stake and a critical role to play in helping to address the challenges now facing the world, contributing to development that is economically, environmentally and socially sustainable.

Sustainable Development and Travel and Tourism

Making Travel & Tourism work for everyone requires the active engagement of all stakeholders - governments, businesses, local communities and the travelling public. While governments have begun to understand the contribution that the industry can make to sustainable development, their record in adopting appropriate policies to encourage sustainable, economically viable tourism is mixed.

For progress to be made, the Travel & Tourism private sector must play a central role. Between the 1992 Rio Earth Summit and the World Summit on Sustainable Development in 2002, considerable advances were made towards sustainability in the Travel & Tourism industry.

Many Travel & Tourism companies have integrated environmental protection into their operations, mitigating their impact on fragile ecosystems and scarce resources. Some companies are also addressing their economic, social and cultural impact on host communities, for example: working with public authorities to ensure that plans for tourism growth are compatible with development goals; actively promoting locally based tourism related businesses; training local people for employment in management positions; educating visitors about local conservation issues; and promoting culturally-sensitive tourism activities.

A wide variety of cross-industry programmes - such as global funds and foundations, eco-labels and certification schemes, codes of conduct, and awards - have been set up to further encourage sustainable Travel & Tourism company practices. The industry as a whole has contributed proactively to the global dialogue on sustainable development, making concrete proposals for how it can help implement Agenda 21.

The response of the Travel & Tourism industry is still piecemeal and change is relatively slow. One reason for this is the highly fragmented nature of the industry, the great majority of which consists of independent small and medium sized businesses scattered across the globe, often running on fragile operating margins.

The real challenge is to move beyond the current ad hoc approach, to evolve new patterns of Travel & Tourism business that integrate social, economic and environmental sustainability and to encourage a vast and fragmented industry to follow suit. In short, what is required is a greater leadership in corporate social responsibility within the Travel & Tourism industry.

Greater Corporate Social Leadership within Travel & Tourism is vital to the industry's future because it will help ensure thriving, attractive and welcoming destination communities that will draw visitors, the basis for long term growth and profitability. Creating a positive environment for tourism in the long term will require the entire industry to adopt responsible, sustainable practices.

Not only is corporate social leadership important for the good of the industry as a whole, it is also becoming a competitive issue for individual companies. Those companies with a reputation for social leadership today will be the winners of tomorrow. Travel & Tourism's corporate social leaders will:

— Be favoured by a growing number of national government authorities and local communities who are prioritizing sustainable tourism that benefits destinations;

— Build brand value and win market share with the growing number of environmentally and socially conscious tourists and other travellers;

— Attract socially conscious investors, improving access to capital and building share value;

— Enhance their ability to recruit, motivate and retain employees, both in destination communities and throughout the organization;

— Be better positioned to assess and respond to risks and opportunities in the market.

A voluntary approach is crucial. To take advantage of what business has to offer - entrepreneurship, innovation, and management capability - companies must be free to choose how they respond to community needs as the competitive market dictates. Attempting to regulate social responsibility would not only be impractical, given the diverse needs of different communities, it would undermine the personal commitment and creativity that fuel it.

Companies that take the lead now will find themselves at a competitive advantage in five years. Incorporating environmental and social issues into the bottom line makes business sense and doing it now will serve shareholders in the long term.

Bringing visitors to some of the world's most remote and pristine areas, Abercrombie & Kent is committed to low-impact, sustainable tourism that protects the environment and benefits indigenous peoples. The Abercrombie & Kent Global Foundation provides long term support for the protection of natural ecosystems. It aims to achieve preservation through the sustainable unification of environmental and economic goals, linking commercial tourism to local conservation programmes.

It provides assistance reserves and parks and surrounding communities and helps to cope with the environmental consequences of man-made disasters. All Foundation projects are conducted in cooperation with local peoples and regional non-governmental organizations. In 2001, $500,000 in support was given for projects in 20 countries on all seven continents. Guests often visit project sites, providing an opportunity for meaningful contact between travellers and residents.

The company has also created a model for ecologically sensitive safari lodging at its Olonana resort in the Masai-Mara region of Kenya. The aim is to share the economic benefits from tourism with the indigenous population, to encourage the preservation of the sensitive habitat. An agreed allocation from tourism revenues is provided to the local community.

As a global tourism company, Accor believes it has a responsibility to care for the local environment where it operates. To fulfil this commitment, Accor has integrated environmental stewardship into its corporate governance and reporting structure. An Environmental Charter and a senior-level Committee on Sustainable Development, headed by a member of the Management Board, guide environmental activities worldwide.

Recently, Accor created a new position of manager for sustainable development to coordinate actions and programmes. Local initiatives are identified and carried out by the staff of individual operations, who are familiar with local issues - more than 800 projects have been initiated to date, in various fields, primarily humanitarian aid and protection of environmental and cultural heritage.

Examples include the A Tree for a Child programme in Indonesia, aimed at helping to alleviate poverty while protecting the environment, and the restoration of the Red Chapel at Karnak in Egypt. The success of each project is measured using indicators developed by outside special agencies. Assessment has shown the projects to be effective and economically viable.

Accor believes that these actions, together with its overall commitment to sustainable development, have both enhanced the global reputation of the group and increased customer demand for its brands. In 2002, Avis Europe launched a major initiative aimed at actively combating global warming, taking concrete steps to ensure that its business is carbon neutral. In partnership with Future Forests, Avis Europe has launched a three-point 'green plan' to offset the carbon dioxide emissions from both its own operations and its car rentals, which has been well received by staff, customers and business partners.

A Europe-wide carbon neutral initiative to offset operational emissions through Future Forests' tree planting programmes. Indigenous trees planted at sites across Europe will re-absorb an equivalent of 32,510 tonnes of carbon dioxide over their lifetime. The world's first carbon neutral car rentals for online customers, in which customers are encouraged to offset their car rental emissions as part of the online booking process.

A target to reduce operational CO_2 emissions from 2003. British Airways has made sustainability an integral part of its business management process. A company-wide Social and Environmental Policy was developed and is published on the company's website. A Sustainable Business Unit was created to oversee activities, provide advice and support, and monitor and measure results.

A senior management level Environment and Social Council has met two to three times per year to discuss policy and strategies and review performance against targets. All activities are published in an annual Social and Environmental Report. The company uses the Global Reporting Initiative guidelines for sustainability and has introduced a code of business conduct for social and ethical accountability. With regard to charitable giving,

British Airways meets the UK's Business in the Community Percent Club criteria and support is maintained irrespective of financial performance. Specific initiatives include:

— The Tourism for Tomorrow Awards, which recognize innovative sustainable tourism projects around the world, and have received wide media attention.

— The Change for Good programme in partnership with UNICEF, in which British Airways customers have given more than £14 million for children's programmes around the world.

— The Communities and Conservation programme, which donates some £1 million each year in travel awards to organizations working on youth development and education, heritage and tourism, and the environment.

Carlson Hospitality Worldwide is committed to supporting both responsible environmental and social best business practices in hotel operations. Environmentally sustainable practices are encouraged company-wide, including water conservation, paper reduction, energy management and employee awareness training.

Carlson Cruises Worldwide is a strong supporter of local charities and surpasses International Maritime Organization standards for cruise ships, employing state-of-the-art water treatment systems. Carlson Restaurants Worldwide assists non-profit organizations that focus on diversity, hunger, children and education, through volunteering and fundraising.

These activities are part of Carlson Companies' long-standing commitment to business ethics and humanitarian community involvement. For example, every year, the company gives five per cent of pre-tax profits to community causes, and it actively facilitates employee community involvement.

In 2002, the Curtis L. Carlson Family Foundation co-founded the World Childhood Foundation, whose mission is to promote better living conditions for vulnerable and exploited children and give them the opportunity to become strong, secure people and good citizens. In 2001, the Carlson Volunteer Connection was launched, an automated on-line intranet system that connects employees with hundreds of community volunteer opportunities in its home city of Minneapolis.

The company has also been recognized for creating an excellent workplace for employees, and in 2001,

Marilyn Carlson received the FIRST Award for Responsible Capitalism. As part of Citigroup's corporate citizenship programmes, Diners Club, in partnership with other Citigroup businesses, uses its financial expertise to help build economic competence and capacity in emerging markets around the world.

All projects are initiated and conducted by local affiliates, with active participation by employees. Three main areas are targeted:

— Financial education programmes that increase people's ability to make informed financial decisions and develop assets - such as a home, small business or an education - that will contribute to family stability, good consumer habits and an increased stake in one's community.

— Preparing the next generation through teacher training programmes in low-income communities and scholarships to increase access to higher education.

— Building communities by helping local financial institutions to construct affordable housing, revitalize low-income areas, make infrastructure improvements and encourage environmentally sustainable practices.

In 1996, a new ownership and management team at Lusotur undertook to transform Vilamoura - of Europe's largest tourism destinations - into an environmentally sustainable resort. A company-wide environmental action programme was adopted at site to monitor and control the environmental impact of all activities - including resource utilization, waste management, staff awareness-raising and stewardship of local natural and cultural heritage - and management structures were adapted to make environmental protection an integral part of operating policies and practices.

TUI is the world's leading tourism group, whose brands include TUI, Thomson Holidays, Fritidsresor, FIRST, Holland International, Lunn Poly, TUI hotels and resorts and the airlines Britannia and Hapag-Lloyed-Flug.

TUI has made environmental sustainability a priority for its extensive network of tourism holdings and destination partners. All activities are coordinated by a Group Environmental Management Department, whose purpose is to ensure that environmental quality management is integrated into every link of the tourism value chain.

Several thousands of TUI hotel partners are monitored in accordance with TUI's environmental quality standards - on energy and water use, waste treatment and conservation - and checked annually for compliance. Awards are used to encourage exemplary practice: the TUI Environmental Champion Award for hotels and the TUI Environmental Prize for community groups.

TUI travel agencies and brochures give customers information about environmentally friendly hotels in destinations and local TUI tour services actively participate in conservation projects, such as reforestation and endangered species protection. All work is conducted in cooperation with experts, government agencies, nature conservation associations and other competent players in the field of environmental management.

Because environmental degradation carries real economic costs and risks for business as well as communities, the company is guided by the conviction that tourism can and should be a leading force for conservation and sustainable development. Uniglobe Travel is the world's leading single brand retail travel franchise company, with 1,000 locations in 20 countries.

Within the Uniglobe organization, the concept of 'franchising' is used to maximize the effectiveness of is community activities. All operating units focus their energy and resources towards a common direction, thereby delivering greater results collectively than could be achieved individually. Efforts are focused on supporting the Easter Seal Society, which helps children with physical disabilities to achieve their full potential and independence.

Within this broad common direction, each region makes a local decision about the extent of its involvement. The company is guided by the philosophy that contributing to society at large is both the right thing to do and good for business because it creates a collaborative organizational culture that is key to retaining motivated employees.

Worldspan provides global electronic distribution of travel information, Internet products and connectivity, as well as electronic commerce capabilities for travel agencies, travel service providers and corporations worldwide. Worldspan President & CEO, Paul Blackney, believes that corporate social responsibility should be a philosophy that permeates the organization and a process in which everyone is involved.

Hence, with the CEO as a catalyst, the company focuses on direct employee participation in community initiatives. To ensure appropriate focus, a dedicated department within Worldspan reviews and decides on each request for assistance or participation. Worldspan programmes address both environmental and social needs. In its home community of Atlanta, Georgia, the company designed the city's largest van pool programme, to help reduce air pollution and fuel consumption, and it is now helping state and local authorities to promote the practice with other companies.

Worldspan also supports the arts, supplies materials, equipment and tutoring to disadvantaged youth at local elementary schools, and funds preferential house mortgages for disadvantaged people. Company employees have helped to build five 'Habitat for Humanity' homes and they participate in walks, runs and many other types of fund-raising projects, benefiting the communities where they work and live.

2

Recent Developments in Travel and Tourism

The travel and tourism sector, while a relatively recent phenomenon in its present form, has been with us for centuries. An extremely insightful comment from Hippolyte Tain illustrates the lack of change in tourism over the past two centuries: "There were essentially six kinds of tourists. The first travel for the pleasure of moving, absorbed in counting the distance they have covered. The second go with a guidebook, from which they never separate themselves: 'They eat trout in the places it recommends and argue with the innkeeper when his price is higher than the one it gives.' The third travel only in groups, or with their families, trying to avoid strange foods, concentrating on saving money. The fourth have only one purpose, to eat. The fifth are hunters, seeking particular objects, rare antiques or plants. And finally there are those who 'look at the mountains from their hotel window . . . enjoy their siesta and read their newspaper lounging in a chair, after which they say they have seen the Pyrenees.'"

While the recent commodification of travel has altered the nature of the travel market it has also given rise to new regulatory problems. The flow of tourists primarily from developed to developed and from developed to developing countries has meant that competition and market structure issues in developed countries have had cross-border effects not previously encountered. Similarly, the trend toward globalization has placed the national and regional nature of the regulatory system under increasing strain.

The key relationship in the holiday industry is that between those who supply the "holiday" package and those who retail these holidays. The supplier, or tour operator, puts together the holiday package by negotiating with destinations and operators in third countries. Tour operators operate largely through the following routes:

— A subsidiary of a vertically integrated firm with a number of related travel interests;

— An entirely independent firm that specializes in putting holiday packages together and selling them;

— A subsidiary of an airline; and

— An operator directly linked to a travel agent.

The tour operator market is characterized by a large number of small players and a few very large players with relatively large market shares, as shown in table 1 below. This tends to lead, in most industries, to a position where the larger operators face little effective competition because the size of the next tier of competitors is so small. The travel agent acts as a broker and retailer of holidays to the consumer. The travel agent is the high street presence that most people think of when they think of the travel market.

Table 1
Tour operator market concentration, United Kingdom and United States (Early 1990s)

	Tour operator numbers	Number of major tour operators	Major tour oper atormarket share (percent)
United States	c.1,500	c.40	c.33
United Kingdom	c.1,000	c.4	c.60

Source: M. Thea Sinclair and Mike Stabler, 1997. *The Economics of Tourism* (London, Routledge).

In the role of broker, the travel agent is presumed, and wished to be, independent of the tour operator. There is an interesting divergence of market structure between the United States and Europe in this last regard. In the United States, around two thirds of travel agents are independent agents without any ties to tour operators or airlines.

In contrast, in the United Kingdom for example, the opposite is the case, with one third of travel agents being independent and two thirds tied. This tying of agents removes the role of the travel agent as a broker and replaces it with the role of sales outlet. This change in role, which is not necessarily clear to the consumer, is one of the key problems for getting destinations to market and in dealing with the market power of those travel agents that are tied to tour operators.

There are a number of developing trends in the tourism and holiday market in developed countries that have important implications for developing country strategies. First, the developed world consumers are taking more holiday time dedicated to the pursuit of relaxation. However, conversely, the time in which they have to research and take decisions about that enhanced leisure time has been curtailed.

Thus, developed world consumers are becoming holiday-rich and leisure-time-poor at one and the same time. This has enormous implications for developing countries in relation to the type of product they offer and the manner in which they make their leisure offer visible to the consumer in developed countries. For example, a notable trend in the 1990s in United Kingdom travel agency bookings is the shift toward later and later bookings.

Fewer consumers are booking holidays a significant time in advance, and more are booking last-minute holidays. This trend, which makes the market less manageable for travel agents and tour operators, does offer destinations opportunities to bypass tour operators to reach into the decision-making process through use of new media.

Secondly, and importantly for developing countries, the number of long-haul holidays being taken by developed world consumers is increasing and showing few signs of slowing down. As table 2 below indicates, the share of total United Kingdom package holidays accounted for by long-haul holidays is small, but increasing. The trend towards greater numbers of inclusive long-haul holidays is aided by the simple fact that the unit cost of getting consumers to long-haul destinations is lower than to short-haul destinations.

The growth in independent holiday-taking has been marked in the United Kingdom since the late 1980s with figures growing by around 40 per cent. However, the division between destinations in this growth is notable. The huge growth in holidays to the Far East/Asia and to the United States has seen up to half of all holidays to these destinations being taken on an independent basis. It appears that destinations less well known to the consumer are much more likely to be accessed on an inclusive basis in the first instance.

Table 2
United Kingdom long-haul inclusive holidays
(Million and percentage of total inclusive holidays)

	Long-haul inclusive holidays	As percentage of total inclusive holidays
1990	1.2	11
1991	1.2	11
1992	1.4	11
1993	1.5	11
1994	1.7	11
1995	1.9	13

Source: International Passenger Survey.

The growth in long-haul holidays from developed countries has essentially followed a two-stage process. In the first stage the long-haul holiday to developing countries tended to be of the cultural and exploration variety. Such holidays appealed to either guided wealthy tourists, or poor backpackers. The more recent stage of growth has seen long-haul holiday destinations offer a competitive product to the beach-based holidays that dominate the inclusive market in Europe.

Such destinations as Thailand, India (Goa) and the Gambia have been able to offer new variations on the package holiday and have managed to tempt the inclusive holidaymaker to travel further afield.

Competition issues in the travel trade

The relation to the airline alliance development, the manner in which competition occurs in markets is a culturally specific process and one that involves an interactive process between the macro-factors of market structure and process and the microlevel factors enshrined in consumer decision-making processes. In the travel trade these two approaches centre inquiry onto the distribution channels by which information is communicated and decisions are made. The implications for developing countries of the manner of competition in the travel trade are twofold:

— How destinations interact with travel channels: supply;

— How travel channels interact with consumers: demand.

The travel trade is the sector that joins these two together. The manner by which the industry deals with either end of the equation is the key to the structure of the market. At the destination end there is a rather simple set of problems for destinations to face. The following factors have to be taken into account: There are relatively few developed country markets that can provide significant tourist numbers:

— Reaching those consumers has always been difficult for individual countries/destinations;

— Developed country firms act as intermediaries:

— These firms are becoming fewer in number;

There are far more countries and destinations available to these potential tourists:

— Access to information about destinations has been restricted;

— Trusted intermediaries have tended to control this information flow;

— Consumers tend to want a limited range of holiday types:

— Destinations differ in what they offer and how they offer it.

The competition issues involved in carrying the consumer to the developing country tourism destination are reasonably soluble through the utilization of negotiation, lobbying and monitoring. However, there is a more difficult competition problem contained in the issues about how the tourism destination in a developing country reaches the consumer. This is not just a matter of marketing and advertising.

There are a number of key competition issues at the demand end of the equation in tourism development that arise from the manner in which distribution channels for tourism products are structured. In particular we need to focus on:

— Physical distribution networks

— Travel agents:

— Unbundled travel packages;

— Bundled travel packages;

— Technology solutions to distribution bottlenecks;

— Generating demand through image control and promotion.

There are many different types of consumer with differing needs and differing levels of incentive to research new destinations. It has also to be noted that individual consumers can have different patterns of demand at different times of the year and throughout a lifetime. The differentiation of the consumer must thus be carried out on a social basis, an age basis (e.g. the "grey market"), a life-cycle basis (e.g. young families versus young singles), a seasonal basis (e.g. summer resorts/ winter breaks) and a time basis (e.g. long/short break).

If one takes this greater differentiation and adds in another complex factor to the equation one can begin to unravel some of the distribution issues that face tourism resorts when trying to reach their prospective consumers. The major factor driving so much of the leisure sector in developed countries is the rather contradictory process that gives workers longer guaranteed holidays, but less time during working periods to find out how to utilize that time.

In essence people are working harder during most of the year, but taking longer breaks for holidays. However, the key day-to-day problem for many consumers is "time poverty". While a large number of consumers are suffering from time poverty, there is another group that is time-rich. The key issue with these two groups is marrying up that distinction with income levels. There has developed a divide between the time-poor/income-rich and the time-rich/ income-poor.

However, there are significant niche markets of consumers who are both income- and time-rich. This group is most likely to be found among retired workers and has been quite effectively tapped by such groups as the Saga Group in the United Kingdom. The distribution of separated travel offerings can occur via a number of routes.

One of the most interesting growth areas in distribution is the Internet. This growth presents significant challenges to existing players and distribution networks. In Europe there is a heavy usage of charter airlines and all-in-one package holidays. In the United States there tends to be much more reliance on direct airline use and associated bookings carried out independently of each other.

The competition and regulatory issues are thus likely to be very different. There are also likely to be more specific strategic issues for developing countries trying to market themselves as destinations in such different markets. For example, in the United States the global distribution system (GDS) used by airlines, hotels and car hire companies is going to be of great importance in shaping the competitive environment within which firms operate.

In Europe, by contrast, the position of the tour operators and travel agents will be of central importance, as they act as portals through which travel choices are put before consumers. For the unbundled travel package the manner in which information is displayed on a computer reservation system (CRS)/GDS is thus centrally important.

The manner by which travel agents are remunerated is also important, particularly when it comes to such things as hotel and car hire recommendations. The tourism destination in the developing world has a dual problem of ensuring that once the consumers are dealing with the travel agent the information is displayed in an unbiased manner. The second problem relates to the need to try to influence the consumers ahead of their initial decision.

The unbundled travel package is as likely to be based around a clear asymmetry of information as the package travel offering. However, it has the initial appearance of not being thus biased. The challenge is thus to bypass the established distribution channels with information targeted at consumers to enable them to deal with travel agents with a more symmetrical distribution of information.

The key problem for both consumers and destinations is the dominance of the travel agent as a purveyor of information and advice. The key issue for the destinations was neatly summed up by the Director-General of Fair Trading in the United Kingdom when he launched the Monopolies and Mergers Commission (MMC) inquiry into vertical integration in the travel industry. He was concerned that vertical integration among tour operators and travel agents would create the "market power to put competitors at a disadvantage, for example by deracking (removing brochures from shelves) or threatening to derack their brochures in an attempt to negotiate larger commissions, by pressurizing tour operators not to supply independent travel agents on better terms, or by pushing their own holidays through in-house incentive schemes".

The importance of transparency in the market is important when one considers how few consumers actively "shop around" in the market for holidays. Evidence from the United Kingdom Consumers' Association (CA) indicates that fully 63 per cent of consumers do not shop around between travel agents before they purchase a holiday.

While this is a concern where links between travel agents and tour operators are not made apparent, the issue of brochure use highlights the scale of the problem. As discussed above, the travel agent "racking policy" (the decision on which brochures to place on display) amounts to the distribution of a scarce resource. For tour operators, the travel agent display rack is almost an "essential facility", where a denial of access can severely restrict consumer exposure.

The same CA evidence indicated that 67 per cent of consumers looked at a number of brochures before deciding on a holiday and 58 per cent of all holidays booked by these individuals were booked on the basis of brochure information. This lack of transparency effectively allows tour operators to restrict the choice available to consumers. The problem here for destinations is that, following the inquiry, the travel industry has become more concentrated and less diverse.

Already large vertically integrated tour operators are combining into even larger groups. While this acts to restrict the transparent choice available to consumers it even more clearly places a constraint on the ability of destinations to "shop around" between tour operators to ensure that they receive a healthy margin and a prime marketing position. This concentration among tour operators, which is currently proceeding at a pace across Europe, threatens to reduce the actual number of tour operators in the market.

This will clearly transfer a good deal of market power into the hands of the intermediaries that direct consumers to specific destinations. This should be a major concern for developing countries. The fact that the larger operators will offer a multitude of differently branded brochures selling everything from beach holidays to escorted cultural tours will look like a wide choice to the consumer. However, both to the destination provider and consumer, the actual number of options will have been limited at the discretion of the tour operator/ travel firm.

This lack of diversity in the sector is particularly apparent in Europe, as the tour operator is in a key position in the travel market. The process of concentration in the tour operator end of the travel business has become more rapid since the MMC inquiry finished its deliberations. The inquiry faced the difficulty, as mentioned above, of identifying specific remedies for an industry in which market share was reasonably evenly distributed among four large players and then unevenly distributed among a host of smaller carriers.

However, the remedies imposed, which centred on information requirements, set off a rash of merger and acquisition activity that has seen the industry change dramatically. The rather perverse situation that occurred in the industry prior to and during the MMC inquiry was that the vertical control of the distribution chain did not significantly increase retail prices, largely because no single tour operator was strong enough to act as a price leader. It would appear that the major groups are trying to remedy this situation.

The latest twist in the tale of the tour operator concentration story occurred in early May 1999 when Airtours announced that it was launching a hostile bid for First Choice holidays. First Choice had been negotiating an agreed merger with Kuoni Holidays of Switzerland. The Airtours bid, which was immediately notified to the European Commission, would leave the merged group with somewhere around 34 per cent of the United Kingdom package holiday market.

This would overtake the current market leader, who have 24 per cent of the market. The overall picture in the sector would leave the top four carriers with 80 per cent of the market. In Europe, the most recent case, that of the merger between Westdeutsche Landesbank, Carlson and Thomas Cook, was decided in March 1999. The merger case relied upon a definition of the market that understated the degree of concentration.

The market defined was significantly broader than it is in reality. The data used, from the British National Travel Survey, covered the entire UK market for holidays, rather than the more accurate, and narrow, definition of all United Kingdom package holidays. The latter is the market in which the firms operate. Even using this survey, the degree of concentration in the market is apparent.

The major problem with the approach of the European Commission in this case was their reliance on unsound data, which underestimated the effect of the merger, and their rather mechanistic view of how the market functions. As a number of competition studies have indicated, the degree of concentration is only one important element of an investigation. What is also important is the degree of difference between players in the market.

For example, if a merger occurs in which the two largest players control 30 per cent of the market, but the remaining market is divided up among a very large number of very small players, the effect will be greater than if there are a medium number of firms of near equal size. In the travel agent/ tour operator market, there are indeed a very large number of very small operators. This merely acts to enhance the anticompetitive effects of mergers among the large groups.

The radical change in concentration at the tour operator end is leading to a proliferation at the retail end of the operation. The lack of transparency in the sector, both accidental and wilful, looks set to increase with the threatened launch of a new low-price "fighting" brand by Thomsons to fend off the Airtours bid.

The launch of the fighting brand is an interesting step given the shortage of upmarket rooms in many destinations and would appear to be relying upon the large number of two-star beds that have been freed up by the difficulties faced by Eastern European tour operators.

The large number of brands, brochures and specific holiday options only serves to drive the consumer into the arms of the travel agent booking clerk, who can then feed the consumer through the travel-buying process. Of course, the lack of objectivity in the computer system is not made clear to the consumer, who assumes that the "best deal" is being offered.

This increased and non-transparent concentration is extremely important for developing country destinations. Rather simply put, the greater the number of tour operators bidding to offer a destination, the more likely the destination is to receive a healthy return; the fewer the number of bidders, the smaller the return. There are essentially two options for developing countries:

— Intervene in competition investigations of proposed mergers and begin a dialogue with competition regulators about their concerns;

— Develop a strategy to bypass established communications channels.

The former option, involvement in competition investigations, may not be as impractical as it may first appear. For example, national tourism offices in developed countries could be charged with monitoring the developments in industry structure in the countries they serve. This may simply involve occasional meetings and a reading of the travel trade press.

It could also involve offices establishing relationships with other stakeholders in the travel business, including consumer groups and independent tour operators. Should an industry development occur that is of concern to the country, a meeting could be requested with the regulatory authorities.

UNCTAD can play a useful role as well in monitoring wider industry developments, providing expert assistance in specific and important cases and dealing with regional and global regulators, such as the European Commission and the World Trade Organization (WTO). The resources that a country would need to expend would not necessarily be significant, as many regulatory processes can be accessed at a relatively low cost and with advice and help from the regulators themselves.

For example, during a merger case involving two tour operators, one could foresee a situation in which a particular developing country previously dealt with two competing networks but was now being faced by one. It would then have a legitimate interest in intervening in the case to ensure that its interests were reflected in the decision.

Developing countries need to identify means of getting directly to the consumer, bypassing the networks of existing relationships. They need not supplant them entirely, but an effort has to be made to reach the end consumer independent of established intermediaries and channels.

The positive side of this latter recommendation is that the technology available to do this is increasingly available, and at decreasing cost. The travel and tourism product is characterized by two major factors.

Firstly, it provides an experience product, namely, a product whose quality cannot be ascertained in advance of purchase but only assessed after consumption.

The second major characterizing factor is the fact that travel and tourism involves a significant information asymmetry on the part of the consumer in relation to the provider of the service.

These two factors lead to two responses by consumers. Firstly, they will rely on proxy measures of performance for the experience product. They will therefore take into account such things as recommendations from friends/publications/television guides and seek both to rebalance the asymmetry in information and/ or trust the retailing intermediary to provide unbiased information.

The most important development in the area of information provision is the ability of consumers in developed countries to access enormous volumes of information about destinations, flights, hotels and car hire offers via the Internet. In addition to the Internet, there is the more recent development of digital television, which may catapult the Internet into the homes of millions of people previously unwilling or unable to use the Internet.

The effect of both these systems on travel decisions and planning is likely to be profound, if a little difficult to quantify in advance. Most specialist consultancies in the Internet field say that travel and tourism is one of the industries most likely to see significant changes in distribution as a result of the Internet.

What is clear is that the Internet and digital TV offer opportunities to developing countries to bypass established distribution mechanisms and formats and place information directly with the consumer. To do this effectively they will have to format the information in such a way as to maximize its impact on the decision-making processes of consumers.

It can easily be seen that the tourism destination has a major say in the fourth aspect of the holiday, and how it handles this process will very much determine the fifth stage. It should be noted that a successful management of the fourth element would also have a major effect on the cost of developing the fifth. The travel market is no different from others in terms of the relative cost of acquiring new customers as opposed to dealing with repeat customers.

Most industries put the relative cost as being 6:1; in other words, attracting a new customer costs six times as much as retaining an existing one. The important stage for most destinations, particularly new ones, is stage, the pre-purchase decision. This decision evolves through a four-step process called AIDA:

— Awareness;

— Interest;

— Desire;

— Action.

The manner in which many developing country destinations generate awareness and interest has often been left to marketing departments of national ministries to determine, and frequently involves global strategies of "Visit X Year". There is also a panoply of other mechanisms by which consumers access this information from magazines to television holiday programmes to general filmed images. The manner in which a country captures the interest generated by such information depends largely on the ability of its marketers to direct desire in the right direction.

While this may seem trivial, it is important to understand in relation to the bypassing of established channels. In order to bypass established communications routes successfully, one has to be able to funnel interest from consumers into a specific source point. Thus one could establish documentary Internet sites based on the country behind the movie.

The ability to do this can be greatly enhanced by using the Internet for transmitting data and using the growth in digital television to direct advertising directly at consumers upon request, while they are viewing a programme or immediately afterwards. For example, digital television viewers should be able to call up information fairly quickly about a country while they are watching a documentary or film about it and then proceed to request further information and even book a holiday.

At the very least they should be able to call up further information about the destination they are interested in. It is important that developing countries involve themselves in helping to develop this sort of information. This is probably best done with established tour operators, as they will have the necessary budgets. However, a well-coordinated information provision will make a purchase more likely than a poorly coordinated one.

The same philosophy applies to Internet sales. While there has probably been an overhyping of Internet commerce, or e-commerce, it is certainly true that the Internet can act as a very powerful tool for developing countries to offer services to consumers in developed countries. Developing countries should develop a series of Internet sites, possibly supplying them via a main portal service, such as Yahoo or Excite, which allow consumers in developed countries to book holidays and hotels from their computer.

The key approach is to provide the consumer with what they want, when they want it. The Internet sites should aim to provide information and practical links on almost every aspect of a possible request. It is considerably cheaper to have one major site with all of the information loaded on to it than to have a network of offices that respond to telephone inquiries.

The potential spin-offs for developing country firms and destinations are many. There is no need for each firm to have a dedicated link; rather, a central point for hotel bookings can be organized. Having Internet sites accessible to developed countries is also important for putting information across to consumers while they are thinking about possible destinations.

Table 3 indicates that the consumer generally learns of travel opportunities from travel agents and from press advertising and brochure information. The importance of the travel agent is further indicated in the following table, table 4, which shows that the travel agent has the most important influence on the consumer of all the possible media. While estimates of the market for Internet and television shopping are prone to exaggeration, it is clear that they will have greater effects in some sectors than others.

Table 3
United Kingdom travel promotion awareness, 1998
(Base = 151 adults; percentage of total and percentage mentioned)

	Where do consumers find out about travel	What types of travel advertising have you seen
Travel agents	60	63
Press advertising	25	68
Brochures	21	46
Magazine adverts	17	54
TV adverts	17	68
Teletext	13	36
Direct mail	11	46
Newspaper inserts	66	39
Door drops	63	26
Radio	60	25

Source: Royal Mail/Mintel.

The retailing of travel products is likely to be significantly affected. Estimates in the United States put current on-line yearly sales of travel products and retail goods at around the $8 billion mark, with 9 million individual transactions taking place. Accordingly to most estimates of on-line sales, some 30-40 per cent of individuals account for 6 per cent of total sales.

Table 4
What advertising influences you when booking travel, 1998
(Base = 151 adults; percentage)

	Does influence	Does not influence	Balance
Travel agents	54	40	+14
Press advertising	15	72	–57
Brochures	25	62	–37
Magazine adverts	14	74	–60
TV adverts	16	73	–57
Teletext	17	72	–55
Direct mail	19	71	–52
Newspaper inserts	5	81	–76
Door drops	2	85	–83
Radio	3	83	–81

Source: Royal Mail.

It might be sensible for developing country destinations to analyse their most important markets/potential markets and assess the degree to which they will benefit from Internet/digital TV sales. For example, Latin American destinations that currently receive large numbers of United States tourists will probably benefit most from Internet-based sales because:

— The United States consumer is the most likely to be connected to the Internet;

— Travel agency relationships are less manipulable in the United States, with most purchasers going for unbundled holidays;

— There is a large untapped market of United States citizens capable of receiving information.

Likewise, in Europe, the markets that currently receive a large number of tourists from Germany and the United Kingdom would do well to develop an Internet sales strategy. For example, given the large established base in computer services, India would be well placed to develop an Internet service for British and German consumers. Such a site could link consumers to travel agents in India who could book hotels and excursions.

The existing growth in Internet usage in India will capitalize on this. The Internet is a very useful tool for a country such as India because of the enormous diversity of travel offers available within its borders. Everything from the simple beach holiday to wildlife trekking and cultural tours is possible. In many ways the diversity of offers makes marketing such a country difficult without a tool capable of allowing consumers to find their way through the myriad options with minimal fuss.

UNCTAD can certainly help in this area by identifying and promoting best practice in Internet site development. It can also develop technical knowledge and help to identify potential host sites that can act as a portal for a number of linked developing country sites.

Competition issues in aviation

The growth in airline alliances is predicated on an essentially unique proposition in global regulatory terms. Most industries consolidate on a global basis through merger and acquisition, or expand through the development of franchising and licensing agreements.

However, in aviation, the development broadly categorized as globalization has been impeded by a number of national, regional and international policy frameworks that have had a significant effect on the shape of the industry and its likely trajectory. At a national level the clearest restraints on airline consolidation come from a few key sources. The source of these policies is not clearly protectionist, although the effect of them may well be so. The key constraints relate to:

- Foreign Ownership Limits;
- Over-flying rights (the so-called five freedoms plus cabotage); and
- National security considerations.

At a regional level there are clear attempts by geographically contiguous country blocs to merge policy in the direction of liberalization within the bloc. Of course the clearest example of this process has occurred within the European Union (EU). However, the dynamic of that process should not be seen as a unique process that cannot be replicated elsewhere in the world. This is particularly the case for developing countries.

If one suspends the notion of the nation-State as the driver in the regulation of aviation and instead thinks of the economic drivers behind the industry, one can see that countries the size of India and China and as geographically dispersed as Indonesia and the Philippines are, in essence, a geographic entity equivalent to an economic bloc.

The pattern of global regulation of aviation competition has emerged very slowly over the past 80 years. As with all regulatory environments, there was an element of time lag in the development of regulations to direct aviation. The first real attempt at regulation occurred in 1919 with the Paris Convention, which apportioned rights to countries to ownership of their airspace. This provided the building block for all future agreements, as it permitted sovereign nations to offer concessions on a reciprocal basis to fellow States to allow aviation to occur on an agreed basis.

Of course, that Convention was fairly limited in scope, as only a few countries had any interest in aviation. However, this purely bilateral approach to aviation began to suffer from the strains of traffic levels and an increase in the number of countries involved in aviation very early on, and by the time the Second World War came to an end, a new approach to the regulation of aviation had begun.

The 1944 Chicago Conference brought together 52 nation-States to discuss the regulation of aviation in three key areas:

- The control of flight frequencies and flight capacities;
- The control of fares and freight charged; and,
- The exchange of the right to fly between countries: the "five freedoms".

The main divisions between countries 50 years ago at the Chicago Convention are illuminating when thinking about the geopolitics of aviation today. At the Chicago meeting the United States took a very laissez-faire attitude to the negotiations. It wanted to see no control of fares and capacities and the most liberal application of flight freedoms.

The primary reason that the United States took this position was the strength of their domestic commercial aviation sector, which had survived the war relatively unscathed. The United States commercial aviation sector had already undergone a process of restructuring that had led to the emergence of the big four airlines, which accounted for 80 per cent of United States domestic traffic by the onset of the Second World War.

The United States was supported in its efforts by, most notably, the Netherlands. This position emerged from the fact that that country's national market was too small to sustain a significant international airline. Instead, the country would have to rely on international traffic for its survival. This positioning was interesting when one thinks of airlines like Emirates and Singapore Airlines: both rely on international traffic and the ability to transit international passengers through domestic hubs that have been designed to maximize spending and stopover opportunities.

On the other side of the Chicago divide stood the United Kingdom and most other European countries.

Given the fact that the ravages of war had effectively destroyed their domestic aviation industries, it is hardly surprising that they opposed total free trade in air transport services. Such a position would have left them open to dominance by United States carriers.

The failure to agree on any truly liberalizing agreement on fares and capacity led to a peculiar situation in international aviation. The Chicago Convention, which was eventually signed at the meeting, was reduced to two elements: the right to overfly another country, and the right to land in another country-the first and second freedoms.

The Convention also led to the establishment of the International Civil Aviation Organization (ICAO), which acted both as a forum for the development of aviation regulation and as a centre for the dissemination of information and technical assistance. It is useful to contrast the failure of the Chicago Convention to establish aviation regulation on a sound footing with the other international regulatory developments that were occurring at the same time.

The impending end of the Second World War and its immediate aftermath led to the creation of the United Nations, the Bretton Woods twins, the International Monetary Fund (IMF) and the World Bank, and the latter's half-brother, the General Agreement on Tariffs and Trade (GATT). Even the least comprehensive of the agreements, the GATT, established a system of important and broad principles for the operation of international economic commerce.

It is instructive to note that the sectors not covered by such agreements included agriculture, shipping and aviation. The mere listing of these exemptions to international regulations indicates the centrality of feelings of national security and well-being to the conduct of international negotiations. The weakness of Chicago led to the three core elements of aviation regulation-fares, capacity limitations and traffic rights-being ceded to different actors in the market place.

The regulation of fares fell to the International Air Transport Association (IATA), a cartel of the international airlines. Capacity limitations became subject to a process of negotiation between airlines (interlining agreements) or between countries on a bilateral basis. The all-important traffic rights became, and have remained, an important issue between Governments, to be negotiated on a bilateral basis.

The increasingly anachronistic nature of aviation regulation has led to a greater incidence of calls for a move toward a multilateral system of governance. While certainly not a coordinated nor deafening chorus, the calls for multilateralization have increased in frequency and volume. The calls for such a move have emerged on the back of a number of developments.

— Firstly, the Uruguay Round of trade negotiations developed the General Agreement on Trade in Services (GATS), which has created a climate within which the liberalization of air transport can be more easily envisioned.

— Secondly, the gradual process of liberalization in air transport has now extended beyond the shores of the United States to reach Europe and a number of significant countries, most notably Singapore and the United Arab Emirates. The possibility of a demandeur for increased liberalization may thus emerge from among this group.

— Thirdly, the trend toward increasingly large "families" of airlines in alliances is posing a challenge to the current system of regulation.

— Fourthly, and not least, the international aviation sector is increasingly seen as an "anomaly" in regulatory terms.

The work at the Organization for Economic Co-operation and Development (OECD) on air transport, while controversial, has helped to build momentum behind discussions of ways to bring the regulation of international aviation more into line with other goods and services. The GATS agreement created an "umbrella" agreement under which sectoral agreements can be slotted.

While air transport, in the shape of traffic rights, was explicitly excluded from the purview of the agreement, the mere existence of the agreement and its review process provides opportunities for debate and fact-finding about the possibility of including air transport. The establishment of the GATS also developed some important principles for services trade which can be extended on a sectoral basis. The forum and the mechanisms thus exist for concrete discussions on liberalizing international aviation.

The gradual liberalization of national and regional air transport systems has also had a significant effect on the shape of the aviation market and the attitudes of players within it. The liberalization process began in the United States in 1978, which led to the deregulation of the United States market, has been replicated in the EU over a longer period.

The result has generally been more efficient airlines, lower fares and a considerably improved market for aviation services. The process that participant airlines have had to go through has altered the strategic thinking of those airlines. This is particularly true of national flag carriers in Europe who have had to adapt to a considerably more difficult operating environment. While this change has been gradual and far from aggressive, it has had noticeable effects on the strategic thinking and planning of airlines in the United States and Europe.

The changing regulatory and economic environment has also increasingly led to the emergence of aviation alliances. The recent emergence of the "mega-alliances" in international air transport is a result of the interplay of factors that tend to be termed "globalization". Of course, aviation is a peculiar sector in many ways, given the fact that it is both driving globalization, by transporting increasing numbers of people and amounts of cargo, and being driven by it.

The forces that have led to firms in other sectors increasingly operating abroad, deepening their internal integration processes and engaging increasingly in outsourcing, technological investment and cross-border operations, are just as prevalent in the aviation sector. The growth of these alliances has posed a number of problems for domestic regulatory agencies.

The growth in alliances is not unique to aviation; however, there are a number of salient factors in aviation that make the alliance issue considerably more important than it is elsewhere. John Dunning indicates that alliances tend to be found primarily in high-technology industries. In particular, he notes that information technology firms accounted for 40 per cent of alliances, with biotechnology representing 20 per cent, new materials development a further 10 per cent and chemicals, 10 per cent.

The main drivers behind alliance formation in these industries were said to be improved market access and structuring (32 per cent of cases), creating technological complementarities (31 per cent) and reducing innovation time (28 per cent). Alliances were thus seen to be occurring primarily in fast-moving and complex high-technology industries where the cost of research was high and increasing, the speed of scientific change was accelerating and cutting-edge technologies were cited in multiple locations. The likelihood of significant new entry was also a factor in alliance formation.

Within aviation the rationale for alliance formation is different, and importantly so. The industry is indeed fast-moving; however, the main rationale for aviation alliances lies in creating complementary networks of airlines that can deliver a more seamless service, to business-class customers in particular. The urge to form alliances is predicated on the fact that the aviation industry suffers from its own version of the Pareto 80/20 rule, where 80 per cent of the revenue for a firm is provided by just 20 per cent of its customers.

In the case of aviation an Air Transport Association study found that, in 1993, 44 per cent of trips on United States carriers were taken by just 8 per cent of airline passengers. The proliferation of aviation alliances can thus be seen as a strategic response to the need to create networks that enable simpler travel for passengers. Of course, in a normal market, firms would engage a range of strategic tools to enable them to carry out this function more effectively.

In some cases firms would establish joint ventures with local players, and in others they would establish directly owned and controlled subsidiaries. In still other cases franchises would be awarded, or entirely new operations created. However, in international aviation one can only really operate one form of strategic response-the alliance. Even if a firm wished to establish a branch of its own operation in a foreign country, it would not be able to do so under existing bilateral traffic rights and ownership rules.

The final element of the international aviation debate is the fact that the issue of aviation regulation has become an anomaly, rather than an accepted part of the regulatory menu. As mentioned before, OECD has undertaken studies of aviation regulation with a view to framing possible alternative routes. At conferences of aviation specialists, the multilateralization of aviation rules is no longer a whispered conversation but has become a real topic of conversation.

Similarly, a number of airlines have begun to look to scenario planning to enable them to comprehend what a truly global market may look like in the future. The importance of alliances cannot be underestimated as a force shaping the future of the air transport sector. However, to comprehend properly the impact that these alliances will have on the shape of global commercial transport one has to view them from two very different angles.

On the one hand, one has to view alliances from a macro perspective, mapping their development and their impact on competition and firm behaviour. On the other hand, one has to comprehend how the traveller interacts with these alliances and how they view the developments in aviation. Both points of view will throw up potential impacts for developing countries.

From a macro perspective, one can see that the alliance network is not an isolated phenomenon. This is to be expected, as it in fact represents a large number of potential strategic responses being shoehorned into a single form of behaviour. They divided airline alliances between those that were "complementary" and those that were "parallel". The complementary alliances were those that involved second-string operatives uniting to challenge a dominant player on a route or an alliance with non-competing airlines merging their route networks.

The parallel alliances were more likely to contain a dominant carrier on a route and involved merging otherwise competing airlines on a route basis. Their study indicated that complementary alliances raised traffic on routes by 10-15 per cent and parallel alliances reduced traffic by around the same amount. Airline alliances can thus be considered to be in a rather ill-formed stage at present. If significant changes were made to the regulation of aviation ownership and to traffic rights one would expect these alliances to change nature quite radically.

Aviation would probably revert to more normal patterns of behaviour for a mature industry. If one looks at aviation alliances from the perspective of the passenger, one gets a different perspective, one that also has important implications for future airline travel. For the passenger the airline alliance offers some potential benefits as well as potential drawbacks. On the plus side, there are better connections between flights operated by alliance partners and the service improvements so often promised with such firm responses.

These can include better lounge access (for frequent flyers), smoother connections and potentially time-savings from schedule coordination and on-lining of passengers. For those who benefit from these improvements, alliances represent a plus, particularly if fare increases either do not take place or are very small. On the downside of alliances for passengers there are a number of tangible problems, most of which tie back in with the categorization of Park and Zhang of alliances as being either complementary or parallel. If parallel alliances dominate routes then fares can increase quite markedly. Such increases will differ on almost a route-by-route basis.

A large number of studies have been carried out of airline entry and exit and the effect this has on fares. As a general rule of thumb, the exit of an airline from a route (the forming of a parallel alliance) can lead to fare rises of between 10 and 20 per cent. The importance of the dominant carrier in this equation cannot be underestimated. For example, British Airways recently announced that it was replacing its Boeing 747 fleet on transatlantic routes with the considerably smaller Boeing 777s. The immediate effect of this will be to reduce capacity on these routes, particularly in economy class.

British Airways will thus be able to increase its yield per passenger. However, the only reason that the dominant carrier on a route can undertake this is that it faces very limited competition from other carriers. It also knows that entry to the route is restricted by bilateral agreement. There are also significant problems for displays on CRS and GDS screens. A significant element of the recent arguments in the European Commission about airline alliances centred on the ability of alliances to flood the first screen of a GDS/CRS with their own codes.

This is particularly important when one considers the oft-cited series of statistics that indicate that 80 per cent of tickets are sold through a travel agent using a CRS, of which 75 per cent will be sold from the first screen and 50 per cent from the first line. The proliferation of alliances is not just a problem in the filling up of screens, but in the ability globally to brand flights that will help to create loyalty of consumers to that brand.

The tying-up of hub airports is also a significant problem with alliances, as most studies indicate that consumers pay a premium on their fares when they fly through a hub airport. The estimates of this hub premium vary between an additional 10 per cent on a ticket price to an additional 35 per cent. The other problem that alliances can entrench in hub dominance is that of gate access.

Consumers naturally like to be able to walk straight from their aeroplane through a covered walkway into an airport terminal. If gate access is a problem for a non-alliance airline, it might end up having to bus passengers from a stand some distance from the terminal. This reduces the quality of the service experience enjoyed by the consumer.

A further problem with airline dominance, which is enhanced by alliance formation, is the ability of airlines in some jurisdictions to offer travel agents volume bonuses and loyalty rewards. Again, this creates a hurdle over which rival airlines have to vault before they can reach the consumer.

If one merges the two views of airline alliances one can identify some specific problems that may be faced in the coming years. A distinct subset of these provides particular problems for developing country airlines and Governments. The fact that both threats and opportunities arise from this development springs from the fact that economic globalization creates two very distinct sets of forces: centrifugal forces that throw competition ever more broadly, often breaking it into its constituent parts in the process, and centripetal forces that pull competition inwards, concentrating it ever more tightly on individual country markets and sub-markets.

Such forces are unleashed differently for factors as diverse as cultural preferences, branding issues, cost allocation and network choice. Both sets of forces are evident in the alliance process. The emergence of alliances presents a particular problem for developing countries, but also a number of rather specific opportunities. The emergence and shaping of global alliances corresponds quite closely to the centrifugal forces outlined above.

Because of the nature of aviation, the scope of competition can be very broad indeed, if it is allowed to be. The alliance process allows airlines to maximize cost-cutting opportunities through a merger of such activities as maintenance and service provision to aircraft. One study indicates that cost savings for such alliances can be quite significant.

Cost-saving is almost always a stated aim in airline alliances. However, such savings can often be difficult to obtain due to the sometimes exaggerated degree of harmony among alliance partners and due to the fact that some major cost savings often involve shedding staff. It is notable that aviation unionization is some way ahead of unionization in other industries. While cost savings can be illusory, the revenue and passenger gains afforded by alliance formation can be very real.

Alliance networks theoretically place competition between airlines on a new footing. In reality such competition actually only exists for a relatively small number of passengers. Very few passengers are likely to benefit significantly from global networks, as relatively few passengers fly on routes/journeys that involve a large number of changes and connections. Most passengers either fly point to point, or connect once to carry their journey to its end.

What airline alliances do is allow all of these smaller point-to-point, or one-connection, journeys to be made with more ease by business passengers in particular. It should be noted that business passengers value their time more highly than leisure passengers. The centrifugal forces that appear to be throwing aviation competition onto a more global basis are countered by some major centripetal forces that are starting to feed through in a number of industries.

The specific centripetal forces applicable in services trade are particularly interesting. Consumers are, at one and the same time, seeking a degree of uniformity in service provision as well as seeking something that is culturally resonant and unique for them. This need not be a contradictory process; after all, it is behind many of the manufacturing platforms in the car industry, for example.

The tension between standardization and customization had led to the emergence of "flexible standardization" in that industry, and it is starting to appear in aviation as well. However, with a few exceptions, it is not being done in a particularly conscious manner. In aviation terms the tension lies between wanting to have the uniformity of safety and service provision and the flexibility/customization of the national culture of the airline being flown. The development of alliances introduces a further challenge for airlines in serving this consumer.

This added challenge provides an opportunity for smaller carriers outside alliances and for niche players within alliances. The airline alliance is a good opportunity for airlines to tap into a network of airlines that will allow them to agree to common standards of service provision. If an airline forms an alliance with a leader in this field, such as Swissair, it can gain a good deal, both in terms of information cross-fertilization from the airline partner and of boosting the image of the airline by association.

Such an alliance can help to provide travellers with the first half of their needs-the uniformly high standards of service and the expectation of that high standard. However, the alliance does pose a problem for the provision of the latter half of the consumer demand-the customization of the service. Just as the hotel sector is finding that consumers do not always want a totally uniform product wherever they go, so the airline industry has to recognize the desire for cultural diversity.

The challenge is to create a service offering that does both-that provides comfort through high standardization, but that customizes this service offering to reflect the cultural diversity of the countries' airlines. If the latter part of the offering is handled badly, the particular image of the airline will suffer. Centripetal forces require an emphasis of diversity on a base of uniformity.

A number of airlines have managed to achieve this heady mix, most notably Singapore Airlines and Emirates. Both have managed to offer that basic level of customer service, in terms of aircraft provision, airport management and punctuality, while boasting a distinct, culturally-specific service offering.

While the Singapore Airlines offering may have been clumsy in its pandering to the fantasies of Western business travellers, it has recently relaxed into a flagship example of how to handle the cultural contradictions in airline travel. There are several potential lessons from this analysis:

— Use an alliance to capture major carrier credibility;

— Negotiate that alliance to avoid losing cultural identity; and

— Avoid alliances and develop a niche market.

All of these strategic responses can be aided by Governments tying tourism promotion efforts more closely into airline marketing behaviour. Both mechanisms should try to reinforce cultural messages and offerings that seek to differentiate the airline from others while assuring travellers that it is just as safe as all the others.

The proliferation of airline alliances has placed the structures charged with regulating them under severe strain. This strain has fallen most clearly on those competition agencies with most alliances on their "patch". The most important regulatory systems in dealing with alliances in recent years are those in the United States and the EU.

The EU system of alliance regulation was effectively kicked into life following the proposal to ally the services of British Airways (BA) and American Airlines (AA) on the transatlantic routes in summer 1996. The EU claimed competency to look at the alliance under article 89 of the Treaty of Rome, under which the European Commission (EC) can express a Community interest in an existing national competition investigation, and duly carried out an investigation of the alliance, the results of which are still pending implementation.

The core issue for the EC investigation was possible breaches of both article 85 (governing horizontal agreements between firms that might lead to dominance of a market) and article 86 (which governs the abuse of a dominant position). In the end the Commission found that the agreement between the two airlines constituted a breach of both articles and needed to be blocked if the proposed remedies were not accepted.

The Commission looked only at those routes where there was sufficient traffic on which to expect competition. Such a route density reliance is a notoriously difficult argument to maintain. The resulting EU analysis focused on the broad range of barriers to competition that an alliance might cause. The central element of the analysis was that, for an alliance of the magnitude of BA/AA, or Lufthansa/ United, to proceed, a divestiture of slots would need to take place and a divestiture that was targeted at creating effective competition for the incumbent carrier.

In both cases the Commission effectively capped the possible market share for each alliance. For BA/AA it was stated that the alliance would not be allowed to hold more than 45 per cent of the available slots on any one route, unless the divestiture of slots would lead to another carrier/alliance gaining such a dominant position.

The timing of the slots needed to be given up was also an important factor in the Commission's findings. The alliances were to give up slots to newcomers within a 60-minute period of the requested time. This was designed to stop the alliances merely giving up slots at "bad" times of the day and thereby limiting the likelihood that a new entrant would survive. The initial basis on which divested slots were to be redistributed to rival airlines indicated the thinking of the Commission as to the nature of airline competition.

The EU analysis also rested on the need to restrain the power of alliance carriers' frequent-flyer programmes by either opening them up to all comers or restricting their applicability. The Commission was not dogmatic on either option, but both indicated the degree of seriousness with which it viewed the anticompetitive effects of airline alliances.

There was also a recognition of the power of CRS displays to restrict competition in air services. The Commission explicitly stated that it was concerned about the possibility of an alliance being able to fill the first screen of a display with double lines for each flight. While not stating exactly what it proposed to do about the situation, it did indicate a desire to limit the display problem.

The Commission also showed its concern about the ability of an alliance grouping to skew travel agent recommendations through generous reward and loyalty schemes. The Commission, in responding to a previous complaint by Virgin Atlantic against British Airways, had registered its displeasure with loyalty schemes operated by dominant incumbents.

The United States approach to international alliances has been much more clearly embedded in a view of international relations and negotiations and centres on the country's desire to negotiate "open skies" agreements. Such agreements effectively deregulate access for carriers from the United States and the other party to the negotiations on international routes. Thus, any carrier can fly to and from destinations in either country.

The United States, it should be noted, does not allow any discussions on cabotage for foreign carriers within its own borders. The requirement that a country negotiate an open skies agreement with the United States before antitrust immunity is granted to an alliance is the cornerstone of the approach, which seems to assume that open skies agreements are enough to satisfy competition concerns.

The United States approach, firmly grounded in international relations and the demands of its national carriers, is unlikely to change in the near future. What may force some change is the pace of change in the country's domestic aviation industry. In contrast to the use of alliances as a mechanism for forcing bilateral openness, United States competition authorities take a much more traditional approach to domestic airline mergers and alliances and have sought to limit their potential effects on domestic markets and consumers.

The approach adopted by United States regulators has been neatly summed up by John Anderson, as follows:

"In the United States, DOT [the Department of Transportation] has the authority not only for approving airline alliances, but also for granting those alliances immunity from the antitrust laws. In determining whetl.er to grant approval and antitrust immunity for an airline alliance, DOT must find that the alliance is not adverse to the public interest.

DOT cannot approve an agreement that substantially reduces or eliminates competition unless the agreement is necessary to meet a serious transportation need or to achieve important public benefits that cannot be met or that cannot be achieved by reasonably available alternatives that are materially less anticompetitive. Public benefits include considerations of foreign policy concerns.

In general, DOT has found code-sharing arrangements to be pro-competitive and therefore consistent with the public interest because they create new services, improve existing services, lower costs, and increase efficiency for the benefit of the travelling and shipping public. As with the other international code-sharing alliances that the United States has approved, DOT officials explained that they will not approve AA and BA's proposed code-sharing alliance with antitrust immunity unless the United States has reached an open skies agreement with the United Kingdom."

The effect of these recent developments on alliances has been to encourage greater scrutiny and public debate on their effects and developments. The general effect in Europe has been to encourage a broader debate about the power of international airlines and to take these views more clearly into account in regulatory debates. In the case of the United States there appears to have been a bifurcation between the treatment of national mergers and alliances, which have been subject to very tight regulatory overview, and international alliances, which have been treated much more as a tool of international relations to encourage more open skies negotiations, while leaving United States cabotage off the table.

For developing country interventions the EU process would thus appear to be the more welcoming. The United States approach would appear to make market power considerations subordinate to opening up of market access. One of the key impediments to an airline operating a service to and from a developing country rests on the ability to access airport takeoff and landing slots.

The central issue raised by slot distribution is how to divide a scarce resource for which, in a large number of cases, demand has outstripped supply. For example, access to London Heathrow and Gatwick and to New York JFK and Frankfurt is severely constrained by demand exceeding supply at peak times of the day.

The manner in which this problem has been dealt with has differed between countries. The effect on developing country airlines has not necessarily been as one would expect, with European airports actually seeing greater entry by developing country airlines. It is important to note, however, that the manner of distribution developed in Europe is currently under review by the European Commission. A public consultation on the matter will occur in the reasonably near future.

In the United States the airline industry, with the acquiescence of all competition and industry regulators, established scheduling committees for all three New York airports-La Guardia, John F. Kennedy and Newark-Chicago's O'Hare and Washington National. This allowed the Federal Aviation Authority to define the number of slots that were to be allocated under the High Density

Rule (HDR) at four of the airports and allocate them through the scheduling committee. The system operated from 1969 to 1985.

The scheduling committees at the four HDR airports met on a semiannual basis and divided up the slots at each airport. The committees were made up of each of the existing carriers and were chaired by a representative from the United States airline industry group, the Air Transport Association.

The system started to creak under the strain caused by the need for unanimity and collapsed completely with the 1981 air traffic controllers' strike. The strike effectively limited the number of slots that were available to be flown. A number of solutions were tried, including bimonthly lotteries of slots and secondary trading of slots. However, none of them worked particularly effectively, for two reasons.

Firstly, incumbent carriers were granted "grandfather rights" for their existing slots. Such rights, enshrined in IATA protocols, meant that an airline that operates a particular time slot has a right to use that slot in perpetuity, provided that it uses it for the majority of the time for which it is allocated. This second factor, known as the "use it or lose it" rule, encouraged airlines to hang on to all of their slots and, in some cases, fly uneconomical routes.

The collapse of the 1969 system under the strain on increased post-deregulation demand for slots and the artificial scarcity problem brought on by the 1981 strike led to an increasing demand for a market in airport slots. Unlike the auction system, the buy/sell experiment, carried out during the 1981 strike and its aftermath, had been a guarded success.

Differentiated lottery pools for passenger carriers, freight, commuter aircraft and others to be dealt with as separate pools for slot allocation and auction. Ring-fencing: slots were to be assigned (by lottery) as being capable of recall to satisfy the essential air service requirement to small communities and for international flights into and out of JFK. The effect of the United States High-Density Rule has important implications for developing country airlines.

Of course one has to separate flights by developed country airlines to developing countries, from flights to a developed country by developing country airlines. If the former increase, but the latter decrease, the overall impact on the tourism market of the developing country may be positive.

For example, the decision by Virgin Atlantic to fly to a number of Caribbean destinations has not enhanced access to major United Kingdom airports for developing country airlines, but has enhanced access by developed country consumers to developing country tourism markets.

The potential competition problem for developing country airlines, however, has been the erection of significant barriers to entry at such concentrated airports. The most immediate barrier to entry has become the cost of owning a slot. The General Accounting Office (GAO) has estimated that in 1996 the cost of a peak time slot at an HDR airport totalled $2 million, and an off-peak slot, $500,000.

As most developing country capitals, at least, are served from such constrained airports, the potential earnings from slot sales are considerable. The incentive for a developing country airline to sell a valuable slot is a factor that will need to be taken into account in the planning of transport and tourism policies, particularly following the Asian economic crisis.

A recent High Court case in which the sale of slots to British Airways by a small carrier flying to the Channel Islands has had a major impact on the likely future shape of slot holdings in London. The judge in the case has effectively legalized slot trading at London airports by sanctioning the move in this particular case. The impact on competition is unclear at the moment, as the ruling has not properly sunk into the aviation community.

The European Commission dealt with the issue of slot-constrained airports in a very different manner from the United States. Regulation 95/ 93 came into force in February 1993 and was due for review in July 1997. The need to clear the backlog of major alliance investigations has delayed the review of the regulation to date. The main object of the regulation was the allocation of slots at "fully coordinated" airports-those airports where demand exceeded supply. Such airports include Heathrow and Gatwick, Manchester, Frankfurt, Dusseldorf, Madrid and Munich. The main elements of the regulation are:

— Grandfather rights: an airline using a slot in one summer or winter season has first claim on that slot in the next equivalent season;

— The creation of the "slot pool": new slots and those lost under the use-it-or-lose-it rule are placed in a pool from which they are administratively allocated;

— Priority for new entrants in slot pool access: 50 per cent of slots placed in the pool are to be allocated to new entrants unless those new entrants decide otherwise;

— Restrictive definition of new entrants: the definitions of new entrants for priority use of the slot pool are extremely limited. A new entrant is:

— An airline with under four slots for any route on the day the slot is requested; or

— An airline requesting a slot for a direct flight between two EC airports where the route is a duopoly and where the airline holds less than four slots for that specific route;

— An airline with less than 3 per cent of all slots at an airport, or 2 per cent at an airport system.

On the one hand, the regulation was designed to help to open up competition on intra-European routes through slot-controlled airports, the most important airports in Europe. On the other hand, they were designed not to totally shake up the system of slot distribution that existed previously, nor the system that was operated through the slot conferences of IATA.

The challenge for developing country airlines, and Governments, is twofold. As discussed in relation to the different distribution mechanisms for reaching consumers, Europe has a thriving and very large charter airline market that serves large, vertically integrated tour operators. The tour operators use charter aircraft to ferry their consumers to destinations that increasingly include developing countries.

The growth of charter routes to Goa in India and the Gambia attests to this. However, it appears that in the United Kingdom in particular, charter airlines are not able to hold on to their entire slot pool, and particularly to expand that slot pool to allow them to fly to new destinations. This poses a problem for developing country destinations wishing to see an increase in charter traffic.

The problem is actually to do with the fact that the existing slot regulation has actually done developing and transition country carriers a favour. Because many routes to transition and developing countries are reasonably limited in traffic volume, they can often enter high-density airports as new entrants. The fact that it has, instead, improved access for non-EU carriers has rankled a bit with regulators.

The competitive environment facing destinations is a complex array of factors derived from the nature of the tourist decision, the mode of choice and the mode of travel. The complex interplay of factors in the travel agency market differs from those in the airline alliance scenario. However, they do share the result that competition among players in those markets is changing significantly as the number of players decreases.

This has important implications for developing country destinations, although the exact nature of the response is not always clear. Given that the competition concerns relating to getting tourists into the country make the position of developing country destinations a complex one, we must now turn to the international hotel sector.

Globally, the international hotel sector is characterized by an enormous diversity in provision. The terrain of the hotel sector is difficult to separate from two important drivers of tourism-the position of the supplier of tourists, and the strategic intent of the authority governing hotel construction.

In the case of the former, the travel agency in Europe, for example, contracts with a multitude of hotels in each destination, negotiates rates for a room and then supplies tourists. Contractually the agency is responsible for the performance of the hotelier and so has some degree of interest in ensuring that standards are met in hotel provision. This acts as a control mechanism on performance.

The importance of planning policies in the development of the hotel sector cannot be overestimated. The pattern of hotel provision will have a significant influence over the development and future of a resort. For example, a resort that is awash with hotel rooms and on which almost all land is built will, of necessity, be a mass market resort which will receive a large number of tourists. It will, however, likely become a mass market for relatively middle- to lower-income travellers.

If hotel development is too tightly controlled, the sector may be starved of resources and the optimal level of travellers may not be reached. Limiting development does have the advantage of limiting numbers and possibly allowing the development of a niche, high-income tourist sector.

The distribution issues that affect airlines in relation to GDSs is replicated in the hotel sector but in a more extreme way. This is simply because the number of hotels is vastly greater than the number of airlines. The number of these hotels that are involved in one of the technical booking systems is thus much smaller. There are essentially three routes by which a consumer can access a hotel in a destination country:

— A hotel distribution system (HDS) tied into a GDS: this allows a hotel booking to be made in the same way as an airline reservation. Most hotels in HDS/GDS links are established international chains. The customer thus chooses a brand;

— A package holiday in which class and associated cost of hotel are the primary factors in making a decision. The actual hotel choice is largely predetermined by the tour operator bulk buying rooms;

— Direct purchase of rooms by individual consumers or through travel agents under direction of the consumer. Such purchases tend to require prior knowledge of a hotel.

Hotel distribution systems come in two main types. Firstly, there is the HDS that is linked directly to the hotel's own booking system and tied into a GDS that can be accessed by booking agents the world over. The second type is a similar system that is one step removed from the actual reservation system but is still linked to the airline GDSs.

Travel agencies account for only 30 per cent of all hotel bookings globally. Individuals and companies drive the remainder. However, the 30 per cent figure underplays the importance of the travel agent for tourism-related bookings. For leisure travel one can discount most company bookings. This leaves a greater importance for travel agents than the initial figure supposes.

The fact that a large part of the hotel market is not accessible via established distribution networks again raises the issue of alternative distribution, most particularly through the Internet and via digital interactive TV. Again, there appears to be a very good case for developing countries to try and corral their independent hotel sector into participating in a central booking system supplied with consumers via the Internet. The potential cost savings of this route are remarkable.

The key problem for the smaller industry player is the asymmetry in information between the hotel and the target consumer. This is analogous to the problem in the proliferation of holiday destinations. In both cases the destination/hotel has an offer to make to a consumer, but no clear way to make that offer known. The key issue is how to unlock that barrier and allow freer communication, or more effective targeting. Within that issue is the central problem of market structure and from that, anticompetitive behaviour.

The response from developing countries and their hotel sectors must be the same as for their airlines and destination marketers. Consumers in developed countries, and those increasingly coming from developed countries, are at the wrong end of an information asymmetry. They are largely ignorant of the destinations to which they wish to travel. They are unlikely to have much knowledge of the airline they fly. They may not know much about the destination or its hotels.

Most importantly, the consumer is looking for someone they trust to provide the information they need, and for a guarantee about expected performance standards. Currently two signifiers largely provide that trust. The first is the brand offered for sale. One of the central elements of a brand is its ability to offer assurance of performance to the consumer.

In the hotel sector, where service is the most important factor, the brand takes on an important strength. This brand can take the form of the specific hotel brand or the through-brand of the tour operator. The latter type of brand is the more commonly associated in the all-in-one package holiday market. The often-unstated assumption is that the travel agent/tour operator would not contract with a hotel unless it met certain performance standards. It is this that the consumer relies upon to assess likely performance.

There is an ideal opportunity here for developing countries alternatively to rate and brand their own services. This need for direct branding can be done for reasons of newness (a new resort or expanded tourism sector) or can be part of a wider strategic effort to garner more of the revenue from the travel system. In either case the developing country needs to establish credibility, or borrow it, from a third party.

On the Internet this can be done through linking up with established sites and signing up for certain consumer protection systems. In the non-Internet world it can be done by signing up with established distribution channels. However, this will be done from a position of weakness and may involve significant cost. A possible way around this would be for a number of developing countries in a region to establish their own hotel booking system.

For example, India possesses a world-famous core of information technology specialists, a remarkable diversity of hotel offerings and relatively few outlets to reach consumers. Neighbouring countries also possess a remarkable array of hotel offerings, but have even fewer outlets for their product. If, through the South Asian Association for Regional Co-operation, the member countries agreed to establish (and wire) the infrastructure necessary for an independent HDS, they would have a product that other HDSs would be eager to have access to.

An independent HDS could then link South Asia hotels to booking agents and to the Internet as a means of bypassing the established channels, capturing a significantly greater share of the revenue generated. If such a venture involved cooperation with recognized players in the Internet industry who signed up for consumer protection measures as well, it might even be able to charge a premium for holiday bookings.

There is growing evidence, from the United States in particular, that consumers are using the Internet as a research tool prior to entering the established distribution and sales channels. They are thus attempting to redress the information asymmetry that is common in many retail sectors.

Developing countries should do their best to help the consumers correct this asymmetry so that they might be more willing to try new destinations. Between them, these two factors enshrine the claim to credibility of the established travel sector. They also act to mask the reality of competition in the sector from the eyes of the consumer.

Towards an Integrated Approach

Tourism is a large and fast growing industry. In 1995 it yielded 8% of the total value of world trade. About 450 million arrivals were counted then (German Federal Agency for Nature Conservation (GFAfNC), 1997). Annual growth rate estimates of tourism are 5.5% to 7.2%. Due to its economic importance, a lot of time has been dedicated and is still being dedicated to research on the phenomena underlying and caused by tourism.

For example, a number of studies is available on the economic and environmental impacts of tourism. However, as more and more is known about the driving forces of tourism, it becomes of greater importance to integrate these aspects. An integrative approach enables accounting for the interaction and feedback mechanisms between the subsystems. An illustration may be useful.

Many countries stimulate tourism development in order to enhance their national economies. However, tourism can grow at considerable speed, sometimes to fast for the national economy to keep up with. This results in financial leakages from the tourism market. Furthermore, tourism can have detrimental effects on the environment, which must be accounted for when stimulating tourism development.

If not, environmental degradation can result in a decreasing destination attractivity, resulting in declining tourist numbers. So, lack of integration in policy measures may result in adverse tourism effects. The World Tourism Organization (WTO) states that tourism is "the activity of people who travel to places outside their customary surroundings and stay there for leisure, business or other purposes for no longer than one year without interruption".

A definition much like the one used by the WTO is offered by Mathieson and Wall (1982): "Tourism is the temporary movement of people to destinations outside their normal places of work and residence, the activities undertaken during their stay in those destinations, and the facilities created to cater to their needs." There is a very important distinction between these definitions.

Whereas the WTO explicitly includes business travellers, Mathieson and Wall state that the workplace is not included in tourism, thus implicitly excluding business travellers. However, if 'workplace' is defined in a narrow fashion, some business travellers can still be regarded as tourists. Business travel should be excluded from tourism.

Tourism is the activity of people who travel to places outside their customary surroundings, their main reason for travel being leisure, and stay there for no longer than one year without interruption. However, we will investigate the magnitude of tourism using WTO-data. So one has to keep in mind that in these cases the WTO-definition of tourism applies.

There are many different types of tourism, for which many different classifications have been proposed. One of these is the following:

— coastal tourism and other water recreation;

— mountain tourism;

— city-tourism;

— rainforest-tourism;

— other nature tourism.

The problem with these categories of tourism is that there are overlaps between them. Mountain tourism, for example, could be perceived as being part of nature tourism, while coastal tourism is quite often accompanied by city tourism. Therefore we do not use a classification of tourism types. However, in the future it will be desirable to structure tourism in a systematic way.

As a structuring tool for analysing the phenomenon of tourism, the Pressure-State-Impact-Response (PSIR) method is used. The fact that domestic travel is more important in North-America than in Europe can be explained by the differences in size of the various nations and states in North America and Europe. People travelling a few hundred kilometres in Europe will often cross a border, and therefore travel internationally, while people travelling the same distance in North America will not.

This also partly explains why Europe has been the largest market for international travels for decades, while North America is responsible for only one-eighth of international travels. It may be necessary in the future to examine the domestic travel/international travel-ratios of different regions or countries more closely, because the impacts of domestic travel may well be significant in comparison with the impacts of international travel.

The size and importance of the tourist industry is not just reflected in the number of arrivals, but also in terms of its financial value. According to the WTO, in 1995 tourism yielded 8% of the total value of world trade, and accounted for 30 % of the value of world trade in the service sector. Especially in developing countries tourism receipts comprise a large part of foreign trade, and tourism provides a large part of employment.

Domestic tourism expenditure is known to be about seven times bigger than international tourism expenditure, but the tourism part of total travel expenditure (which includes business travel expenditure, in correspondence with the WTO-definition of tourism) is not known. That is why we can not estimate the total volume of tourism receipts the way we did for the total volume of tourism arrivals.

The WTO distinguishes six world regions: Europe, the Americas, East Asia and the Pacific, the Middle East, Africa and South Asia. In the future it will be desirable to separate the Americas-region in North America and South America, because of their different social-cultural, economic and ecological situations (for example, South America is more important for global biodiversity than North America (World Conservation Monitoring Centre (WCMC), 1994)).

This development can be regarded as the result of trends in basic macro-level factors. Those macro-level factors can be divided into seven classes:

— Technological developments

— Economic developments

— Demographic developments

— Institutional developments

— Political developments

— Cultural developments

— Environmental developments

It is important to note that macro-level factors influencing tourism can be classified in many different ways. In general, technology serves in making tourism more easily accessible by lowering tourism product prices. A very important technological development was the invention of the jet engine. It increased the possibilities for long-haul travel, thus answering to a need long not addressed.

Developments in computer and communication technology are important too, for they increased efficiency in data-processing, lowering the need for administrative personnel, and made information on travel possibilities more accessible. Because of this, travel agents could make reservations for tourists far more easily.

Economic developments in Tourism

Economic development and tourism development often occur in a parallel fashion. Rotow distinguished five stages of economical development, which Cooper et al linked to certain levels of tourism development:

— *Traditional society*: this stage is characterised by poor health, high poverty and low per capita output. Most of the undeveloped world's economies are in this stage. Apart from domestic visiting friends and relatives, tourism does not occur.

— *Preconditions for take-off*: before the economy can change, a certain change in ideas has to take place. This change has to be recognised by the leaders of the country. It is the first step of economic development, resulting in changed economic and social conditions, which permit a rise in domestic tourism development, and the start of inbound international tourism. In other words, this socio-economic change permits the country in question to become a tourist destination. Also, it is important that such a change in ideas could be regarded as a cultural development.

— *Take-off*: the change in ideas mentioned in the 'preconditions for take-off'-stage leads to actual economic changes, resulting in the expansion of manufacturing (which itself results from technological developments) and services. Inbound tourism keeps growing, and the country itself starts generating more and more tourists.

— *Drive to maturity*: economic development results in continued industrialisation, and a shift from heavy manufacturing to more sophisticated and diversified manufacturing.

— *High mass consumption*: at reaching this stage an economy is full-grown, which is characterised by the production of large amounts of consumer goods and services. The country is a major generator of international and domestic tourism. The developed world-economies are in this stage of development. In short: the undeveloped world is not participating in tourism; the developing world starts functioning as a tourist destination, and, as economic development continues, generating tourists itself; the developed world is a full grown tourist generator.

Economic influences are exerted through personal discretionary incomes (income minus tax, housing and basics of life). When assuming that economic crisis lowers discretionary income, crisis episodes should be reflected in tourist numbers. In 1984 tourism recovers. These trends parallel the 1979 oil-crisis, which made oil-prices rise extremely, followed by the economic recession in 1980.

The oil-prices are exceptionally important for tourism, for most of the world's transport systems are dependent on oil-derivatives. The influences of these economic developments are most pronounced in the Europe tourism figures, but appear also in other world regions.

Demographic developments pose a major influence on tourism. For example, predominantly rural nations have low travel propensities, whereas predominantly urban nations have high travel propensities. Very important is the fact that highly urbanised areas with high population densities indicate high levels of economic development and high purchasing power. Age distribution within nations is another major demographic influence. At different stages in life people pursue specific travel experiences (which are also driven by past experiences).

Thus, a baby-boom cohort in a population has an effect on the integral tourist behaviour of that population. These effects are closely linked to demographic transition. Theory of demographic transitions uses four phases to describe changes in population during a country's development:

— *High stationary phase*: high birth rates, high death rates, with a low, stable population. This phase applies to most undeveloped countries.

— *Early expanding phase*: as a consequence of improved health care death rates fall, resulting in rapid population growth. The country starts functioning as a tourist destination, though no tourists are generated.

— *Late expanding phase*: after death rates have fallen, birth rates start to fall too. The end of this phase parallels the economic drive to maturity. The country starts functioning as a tourist generator.

— *Low stationary phase*: low birth rates, low death rates, with a high, stable population. This phase applies to most developed countries.

Institutions can regulate tourism both in the generating and the destination country. For example, in the generating country the distribution of income is very important. When assuming a threshold discretionary income is needed for tourism to occur, a country with a very skewed income distribution will generate less tourists than a country with evenly distributed income.

Furthermore, income distribution is related to the political regime governing a country. Predominantly socialist regimes often have special regulations to provide holiday opportunities for the people in the lower socio-economic classes, whereas predominantly capitalistic regimes do not. In the destination institutions also affect tourism. Some countries regulate tourism by demanding visas and passport-checks. Another example of a tourism regulation is tax on travel.

Bhutan uses an extreme form of tourism regulation. Bhutan started being a tourist destination in 1976. However, the government feared conflicts between tourism and the social structure of Bhutan, and the environment. In order to prevent those conflicts from happening, Bhutan restricted the number of international tourists, from 2000 a year in the early 1980's, to 5600 in 1995.

Political instability is a major influence on tourism too. Countries with wars going on, or countries with a great potential of war are not suitable tourist destinations. The Middle East provides a good example of this phenomenon. Whereas tourism development in, for example, East Asia and the Pacific and the Americas is fairly steady, tourism development in the Middle East fluctuates considerably over time.

This is in correspondence with the political instability in the Middle East, contrasting with the relative stability of East Asia and the Pacific, and the Americas. One such instability is provided by the Gulf War in the early 1990's. World numbers of tourists declined too in 1991. However, it is important to note that these also may be the effects of chance over time.

After the low stationary phase of demographic transition is reached, socio-cultural developments heighten travel propensities. Some of these could also be regarded as being demographic changes. For example, a rise in the percentage of women in the workforce results in a rise in discretionary income. Also, women start having children at a higher age, which changes travel behaviours (the presence of children sets a limit to possible destinations).

In other words, women's emancipation is an important cultural factor. Other developments are increased flexible working time and paid leaves, which enable people to travel more often. This also holds for earlier retirements. Another major influence on tourism is exerted by fashion. A good example of this effect is the popularity of sunbathing. In the past (nineteenth century) a suntan was associated with a working man's life, so people favoured a white tan. This made sunbathing very unpopular. Yet in today's Western culture having a suntan indicates wealth, because 'travelling to the sun' is supposed to be done by the richer people.

The environment can be regarded as tourism's resource base. This implies that environmental developments affect tourism. A good example of this effect is provided by algae blooms in the Adriatic Sea. Tourism suffered from the algae blooms, for the water became unfit for swimming purposes. In the future global warming, and related issues may have an effect on tourism development.

However, the uncertainty around these subjects prohibits a solid view on the effects of these developments. An explanation for this development in world tourism might be that Europe, partly representing a totally developed group of countries, has lower tourism growth rates than East Asia and the Pacific, which are still developing groups of countries. Interestingly this development parallels the rapid development in East Asia and the Pacific, as opposed to the relatively low economic growth rates in European countries.

Clearly, Africa, South Asia and the Middle East are still at the beginning of developing a tourist destination status. Only 24% of the international travellers in South Asia is South Asian, whereas 87% of the international travellers in Europe is European. This might be attributable to the fact that Europe is more developed than South Asia.

The tourism product is a complex mixture of services (e.g. aircraft seats, hotel rooms) and goods (e.g. food, souvenirs) which are bought by a special kind of consumers, namely tourists. Apart from the consumer behaviour approach we also use aspects of personality to describe travelling behaviour.

Jager et al have developed a conceptual model for consumer behaviour. Applied to tourism this model can be used to assess reasons for travel. Jager et al argue that consumer behaviour is the result of three factors:

— *Motivation*: Motivation is created by psychological needs.

— *Opportunity*: The availability of factors that create the possibility for gratification of psychological needs.

— *Ability*: Personal skills and resources needed to use the opportunities. Applied to tourism, motivation is represented by social, ego and self-actualisation needs.

Tourism is an opportunity to fulfil these needs. For example, one might climb Mount Everest in order to gain esteem, which is a part of ego needs. The tourist must also have the ability to use the opportunity. For example, one needs a lot of money to climb Mount Everest, which means that few people have the ability to use the opportunity of climbing Mount Everest.

Krippendorf distinguishes eight reasons for travel:

1. Recuperation and regeneration; people get tired during working weeks, and use vacations to replenish their 'bodily and mental strength'.
2. Compensation and social integration; tourism compensates for everyday social failure by presenting another world next to everyday dreariness.
3. Escape; everyday life contains more and more aspects of stress; people want to escape from this.
4. Communication; travelling abroad gives people a chance to gain human warmth, to establish contact with other people.
5. Broadening of the mind; people want to satisfy their interests in other cultures and nature.
6. Freedom and self-determination; tourists are in a position to largely make up their own rules; they are free from any obligations.

7. Self-realisation; an unfamiliar and strange environment offers a great chance for investigating and enhancing the Self.
8. Happiness; vacations are highly associated with joy and pleasure, so happiness becomes a reason for embarking on a holiday trip.

Furthermore, following the above reasons for travel, tourism seems to serve psychological needs. Nickerson too argues that deep psychological needs are the basic motivators for tourism. Maslow distinguished five different levels of psychological needs ranging from physiological needs to self-actualisation. According to his theory, satisfaction of people's basic needs is a prerequisite for the satisfaction of the higher needs.

Maslow argues that all behaviour is motivated by psychological needs, for behaviour serves to fulfil those needs. Applied to tourism, social and ego factors influence people to travel in order to gain social acceptance and admiration in their social environments. For example, in the Western world people who are not able to go on a holiday trip are often pitied. So, a reason for travel could be the avoidance of pity. Another example is provided by the process of conformity.

If all people in a person's social environment are apt to travel, the social pressure on that person to travel is high. Fashion plays a role too, partly in being part of the conformity process, partly in being a determinant in choosing a travel destination. Jager et al, in their Motivation-Opportunity-Ability (MOA) approach to consumer behaviour, do not use Maslow's hierarchy of needs to describe motivation. Instead, they propose Max-Neef's description and classification of human needs.

However, both Maslow's and Max-Neef's theories aim to describe the same phenomenon, and therefore both offer a starting point in modelling human needs. Although Jager et al state that Max-Neef's theory is more sophisticated than Maslow's hierarchy of needs, we propose Maslow's theory, for it does serve our purposes, it fits the MOA approach, and is also used in Nickerson's theory about tourist motivation.

Opportunities are products and services one can use to fulfil one's needs. In this case tourism is the need-satisfier. According to the theory one's need can be satisfied by many different opportunities. This is in line with the existence of the many different tourism types and needs. There were five different types of tourism—coastal tourism and water recreation, mountain tourism, city-tourism, rainforest-tourism and other nature tourism. These can be regarded as five different opportunities to satisfy one's psychological needs.

Of course, those five types of tourism can each be divided into smaller types of tourism. In repeating this, one would end up having single destinations as tourism types. This implies that each destination is an opportunity for satisfying one's psychological needs, yet specific needs and a specific personality lead to a specific ranking of destination. In exploring the relation between needs and opportunities, five types of satisfiers can be discerned.

An interesting one for tourism is the inhibiting satisfier, which satisfies one need, but inhibits the satisfaction of other needs in the process. Especially interesting is the interpersonal need inhibition. People who seek to satisfy their esteem needs by visiting a certain destination are dissatisfied by other people seeking the same satisfaction or the satisfaction of social needs.

On the other hand, people seeking to satisfy social needs are more satisfied when other people come visit the same destination. So, people seeking satisfaction for some need, may in the process inhibit, and simultaneously stimulate, another's need-gratification.

The phenomenon of the need inhibiting satisfier can explain the pleasure periphery, which describes the spatial spreading of tourism, initiated in Western Europe and North America, across the globe. After the elites or first-movers have reached a new destination, they are often soon followed by growing numbers of emulators.

In turn, this crowding leads the first-movers to recognise that the destination is not a good opportunity anymore to satisfy their esteem needs. So they move on to even more remote areas. The tidal wave of tourism has recently reached Antarctica.

Each opportunity demands a certain set of resources. Individuals (or households) not having these resources at their disposal are not able to make use of certain opportunities. To return to our Mount Everest example, one needs a lot of money to even travel to Mount Everest. Second, one needs great climbing skills to climb Mount Everest. A lot of people do not have those resources (money and climbing skills) at their disposal.

Jager et al distinguish four different kinds of resources:

1. *Physical resources:* These resources refer to people's physical state (e.g. health, strength), and to physical tools and circumstances (e.g. a car, space for storage) people have at their disposal.

2. *Permitted and licensed resources*: Many opportunities demand having certain permits and licenses available. Examples are drivers licenses and educational grades. Limits to these resource are set by the earlier mentioned political and institutional factors.

3. *Financial resources*: These resources refer to income. The higher the income, the more opportunities a consumer can use. On a macro-level this ability is provided by a certain level of economic development.

4. *Social and cognitive resources*: This category of resources comprises knowledge resources, cognitive capacities and skills, attitudes, values and norms.

These resources determine whether someone can foresee outcomes of opportunity-use. Demographic and cultural factors exert a certain influence on this kind of resources. As stated before, motivation, opportunity and ability are not the only determinants of tourist behaviour. Personality influences travelling behaviour too. For example, people who want to climb Mount Everest in general have certain personality traits in common.

Most of those people will have a tendency to sensation seeking, for climbing mountains is performing risky behaviour. Nickerson and Ellis use four personality dimensions to describe tourists in order to indicate motivations for different types of travel:

— Activation: A guest's level of excitement, alertness or energy.

— Variety: The need for change or novelty.

— Extraversion or introversion: The extent to which a person is outgoing and uninhibited in interpersonal situations.

— External or internal locus of control: The way people perceive whether or not they themselves are in charge of the happenings in their lives.

Different types of travel can be regarded as specific types of opportunities. In other words, Nickerson and Ellis link personality dimensions to preferred opportunities. The personality dimensions used by Nickerson and Ellis are commonly used in personality psychology. Therefore it seems relevant to explore a few basic aspects of these theories.

The concept of locus of control was worked out by Rotter. It is a personality trait describing the perceived determinants of rewards and punishments. At the one extreme are people who believe to be in control of their lives (internal locus of control), at the other extreme are people who believe factors like chance, luck or fate are determining the events in their lives. Interestingly, Maslow argues that self-actualisating people have an internal locus of control, whereas people lower on Maslow's pyramid (e.g. social and ego needs) have a more external locus of control.

The introvert-extravert dimension is very popular among trait personality psychologists. Nickerson and Ellis regard sociability as being an important aspect of extraversion. As the activation and the variety dimension are covariant, it seems legitimate to regard them as one. Nickerson and Ellis emphasise a traveller's level of excitement, alertness or energy, and his need for novelty and change, whereas sensation seeking is defined as the tendency to seek out varied, unusual and exciting stimuli.

The Mount Everest climber might best be described by the private explorer tourist type. Beside destination preference Nickerson and Ellis also argue that travel personality is a determinant of interaction with local cultures, degree of activity, and preference in type and number of travel companions, which in turn are determinants of opportunity preference.

Economic Impacts

Many governments see tourism as a facilitator for economic growth and as a source of foreign currency. Tourism is also expected to stimulate employment. These expectations are understandable, given the enormous magnitude of tourism flows on a global scale. However, most of these flows are calculated in gross terms. Net economic tourism benefits for an individual destination are not so easily calculated.

The initial spending of tourists is at the start of the economic chain. Tourists can buy tourism products or services either directly or indirectly. In turn, these products and services can be provided either inside or outside the destination country. Having received the initial spending by tourists and tour operators, the tourism industry in its turn spends this extra income on inputs (consumption) and on the payment of the production factors, labour (wages), capital (interest) and entrepreneurship (profits).

Clearly, tourism can generate jobs. Local people are able to earn their wages and salaries in the tourism industry, either by providing tourist accommodation or by doing business with tourists, like being a tour guide or a food supplier. The actual number of jobs depends on many things, such as the labour intensity of the tourism industry.

In Costa Rica, labour intensity in the accommodation business is heavily scale-dependent. Investments per job are more than three times as high for larger-scale hotels (more than 40 rooms) than for small hotel businesses. The net employment contribution of tourism also depends on crowding out effects on the labour market. For example, people previously involved in agricultural production may accept a better paid job in the tourism industry. While this means production growth in the latter sector, it may mean a production decrease in the former.

As tourism usually displays seasonal cycles, employment in the tourism industry is often seasonal. Moreover, most of the jobs created by tourism are low paid and low skilled. This can have adverse impacts on economic and social stability. Crowding out effects occur not only on the labour market, but on other markets for production factors as well.

Competition for financial, human and natural capital increases, often resulting in a rise of real estate prices and an (increased) shortage of investment capital. Such developments may be detrimental to other economic activities and thus result in structural economic change.

The owners of the production factors spend their income on consumption, savings or taxation. Savings and taxation can be seen as leakages from the spending cycle. However, these leakages are usually only temporary. Savings are simply postponed consumption, while part of tax revenues flow back into the economy in the form of government expenditure.

The importance of repatriation depends to a large extent on the involvement of foreigners and foreign companies. Leakages through repatriation are usually small when employees are local people and tourism companies are owned and financed by nationals. In some developing countries, a large part of tourism income is earned by western employees.

In Tunisia, half the total wage volume reportedly is accounted for by management personnel. Jobs held by expatriates tend to be the more favourable ones, being higher-paid. The money earned by expatriates leaks back to their home-countries. The extra consumption expenditures from buying inputs and from spending production factor income can be directed towards imported products or locally produced products. A large percentage spent on imports means a large import leakage, influencing the balance of payments.

According to France, when the tourism industry is relatively small, food and labour demands by tourism can be fulfilled by the local community. Yet as the tourism industry is growing bigger, the destination country cannot keep up with tourism development. It has to import products from other countries, thus creating a second leakage. It is good to remember that the net contribution of tourism on the balance of payments depends not only on initial spending, but also on the magnitudes of the import leakage and the repatriation of money.

A good illustration hereof is provided by the tourism development in Africa, where rising tourist arrivals are not accompanied by subsequent rising tourism receipts. Increased demand for locally produced goods can have negative consequences as well. Tourists and business-people engaged in tourism tend to have more money than the local community of a destination country, especially in Third World-countries. This is a reason for retail prices to rise during the tourist season. Combined with crowding out effects on markets for production factors, this may inhibit participation of local residents in the local economy.

Now, the amount of money spent on locally produced goods enters the spending cycle again. This amount is, of course, smaller than the initial expenditure due to the various leakages. After having gone through the spending cycle for the second time, less money remains still and so on, until the effects of the initial expenditure have vanished.

The cumulative effect of the initial tourist expenditure going through various spending cycles is called the tourism income multiplier (TIM). The leakage percentage of total tourist expenditure, and thus the TIM, differs greatly between countries. For example, the island Mauritius has net foreign exchange earnings of only 10 percent, compared to 80 to 90 percent in countries like Tunisia or Kenya. A possible reason for this difference is the fact that Tunisia and Kenya only need to import luxury goods to meet tourist demands, while Mauritius is almost totally dependent on imports.

Apart from the recycled initial expenditure from the first period, new tourist expenditure enters the system as well. If business opportunities are good, investors may enhance this expenditure flow.

Leakages from the economy of the destination area are represented by dotted lines (the arrows towards savings, tax, repatriation and imports). Recovery of tax and savings leakages are depicted by the smaller dots. The magnitude of leakages is very much dependent on the scale of analysis. On a global scale, there are no leakages.

The actual measuring of the monetary flows associated with tourism is very difficult, the more so as there is no agreement on the methods to be used. The World Tourism Organisation is currently developing a standard method of measuring the economic impacts of tourism by using satellite accounts next to the existing national accounts. It is important to follow the WTO's proceedings, for they may greatly enhance the possibilities of assessing the economic contribution of tourism and of designing alternative policies.

The net contribution of tourism to a destination's economy depends largely on the spending leakages. If much of initial tourist spendings leak away through imports, taxes and repatriation of profits and wages, net receipts may very well be small.

Environmental Impacts on Tourism

The environment plays a vital role in the tourism industry. Among other things, it serves as an attraction and as a sink for waste residuals. In order to assess tourism's impacts on the environment one can take various viewpoints. One can use a tourism typology and see what impacts are related to the different types of activities. Or one can use an impact typology and see how tourism influences the different types of impact. There were two types of environmental impacts of tourism:

— emissions to air, water and soil

— changes in biodiversity

The first category deals with changes in the abiotic environment, while the second one deals with biotic changes. Obviously, these two are related. For example, emissions can change ecosystem conditions, resulting in changes in biodiversity.

Tourism activities emit waste to all environmental compartments, being air, water and soil. The most apparent tourism-based emission to the atmosphere is caused by transport. In the case of international tourism, this transport first of all involves the movement of the tourist from the country of origin to the destination country. Because tourists cover ever larger distances, emissions grow.

Moreover, a change in travel distances influences the choice of transport mode (modal split), favouring the aeroplane. Apart from this long haul transport, tourism triggers other types of transport as well, such as the movement of tourists inside the destination country and the transport of goods needed to support the tourists.

Clearly, transport is not the only source of emissions. The heating of accommodations and swimming pools and the use of snow machines are other examples of the consumption of significant amounts of energy. From a global point of view, the most important consequence of these emissions may be their contribution to global warming.

The greatest tourism impact on water resources is sewage. First of all, sewage disposal causes water pollution through the usage of chlorine-based cleaning agents, which threaten marine life. Second, in many tourism destinations sewage systems are malfunctioning, resulting in emissions of untreated sewage water to the environment.

Often, sewage problems occur when tourism flows grow faster than the underlying supportive infrastructure, including sewage systems. Emissions of sewage induce eutrophication, which poses a threat to coral reefs, and can induce excessive growth of algae. Algae bloom has occurred in many places, such as Adriatic Sea-coast and the Cancún-area in Mexico.

Nowadays, water quality is constantly monitored in these areas, largely because of its importance for tourism. Some other direct emissions to the aquatic environment are related to special types of tourism, such as boating. Oil leakage can have severe impacts on water quality and its aptness for human use.

Litter is probably the most important emission of tourism to the soil and certainly the most visible. The problem of tourism-/recreation- induced littering is very old, as is illustrated by the ancient Dutch imperative: "Laat niet als dank voor het aangenaam verpozen, de eigenaar van dit bos de schillen en de dozen." (Do not leave, in gratefulness for your pleasant stay, your boxes and litter to the owner of this forest.)

Biodiversity can be defined at three levels:

— the variety of genes per species;

— the variety of species per ecosystem

— the global variety of ecosystems.

Tourism affects each of these levels. At the positive side, it may contribute to more protection of species or ecosystems. The entrance fees tourists pay to visit natural areas can be used for better maintenance and protection. Often, maintenance of natural areas is paid for by the government in the form of subsidies. In many (developing) countries these subsidies are under constant pressure, which makes good maintenance difficult.

In the protected Osa peninsula in Costa Rica, for example, poaching and gold seeking with the use of harmful chemicals are real problems due to lack of staffing. This contrasts with the privately owned Monteverde, which is well-protected and operates at a profit, thanks to tourism. Furthermore, tourism can trigger a change of attitude inside the host country, which may increase the value that people attach to the protection of natural systems.

The most direct way in which tourism affects the abundance of a species is through hunting and fishing. Each animal contributes to the gene-pool of a species, maybe even representing unique types of a gene. Extensive hunting has already led to the extinction of species. A lot of species are currently endangered as an effect of hunting.

Other direct impacting tourism activities are plant-picking and -uprooting, which cause loss of vegetation. Somewhat more indirectly, tourists can influence the number of individuals of a species by buying biotic souvenirs, thereby triggering hunting activities by the local population. Exemplary are the trade in ivory products and products made of crocodile skin.

Perhaps the cutting up of natural areas by the construction of infrastructure also falls into this category. It makes the exchange of genes more difficult, thus hampering the formation of new genetic combinations. Breeding and mating can also be hindered by the noise and the mere presence of tourists.

Impacts on the variety of species per ecosystem Tourism changes ecological processes and will thereby modify the species variety of an ecosystem. Well known are the effects of tourism on soil compaction and erosion. Soil compaction involves the process in which soil particles are pushed together by pressure. Compacted soils have a less abundant bacterial life, and bigger soil creatures are expelled from the compacted soil.

Moreover, compacted soils can hold smaller amounts of air and water, which means that they are less favourable for certain plants (decrease in soil vegetation), and that their surroundings are more prone to water erosion. Morera and Garcias report soil compaction along nature trails in the Monteverde Cloud Forest Preserve in Costa Rica. This soil compaction was one of the reasons for limiting the daily number of visitors to 100.

Unfortunately, hotel capacity in the area had already grown to about three times this number, indicating a lack of integration of economic and ecological developments at the level of policy making Tourism can also have an impact through habitat and ecosystem destruction.

For example, turtles, which have sand beaches as a breeding place, are expelled when those beaches are used for tourism purposes. This is happening in the Costa Rican natural reserve of Tortuguero, where more and more hotels are built at the beaches used by turtles. Turtles are very susceptible to light, so their breeding at the Tortuguero beaches is threatened by these developments. The affected species can even be homosapiens. Tourism affects drinking-water resources.

Tourists use drinking water to take showers and baths, etcetera. In some cases tourists use much more water than the destination area can offer. For example, in the area around the biological reserve of Gandoca-Manzanillo in Costa Rica improper tourism planning led to water shortages for the local population. An example of more indirect tourism interference with ecological processes is the earlier mentioned eutrophication of water resources.

The abundance of nutrients favours the development of some species (algae), while being detrimental to most other species. Oligotrophic ecosystems are very vulnerable to eutrophication. Eutrophication often hinders organisms living in oligotrophic environments, such as coral reefs. Of course, nature can handle an amount of organic waste before eutrophication causes composition shifts.

For example, mangroves and marshes often remove a lot of organic matter from the water, thus leaving coral reefs downstream water relatively poor in nutrients. However, nature's cleaning capacity is limited. Another example are the effects of littering. Bears in national parks have been observed moving to places frequented by tourists. Litter left by tourists also presents a great rat habitat.

Sometimes entire ecosystems are wiped away by tourism. Building new hotels near the seacoast is an example of an activity that can destroy transitional ecosystems between land and sea (for example, dune ecosystems could be destroyed in such ways). Coral reefs are often used as building material, for it is easy to get and cheap. Sometimes reef flats next to coral reef are transformed into airports.

Introduction of tourist infrastructure often involves the relocation of soils, sometimes destroying whole ecosystems. Evidence for such large relocations of soil can be found in Costa Rica. In the Tambor-project, comprising the construction of 1500 new hotel rooms by a Spanish hotel chain, large amounts of white beach sand from another beach were used to cover the black sand of the beach in front of the new tourist resort. The sand used for other parts of the project was obtained by digging off large parts of a riverbed.

The actual environmental impact of a given tourist depends on many factors. The tourism type a tourist participates in seems to be of great importance. Possibly each tourism type has it's own specific detrimental effects on the environment. Furthermore, it is possible, given someone's personality, motivation and ability, to assess the tourism type someone will get involved in. Thus, the MOA-personality approach should, when linked to specific tourism types, be able to infer a tourist's contribution to environmental problems.

Tourism can have important impacts on both the biotic and the abiotic environment. Abiotic impacts arise from emissions to air, water and soil, while biotic impacts are caused by tourist activities such as hunting and processes such as changed land use. Operationalisation of the described method of linking tourism type, tourist type and environmental impacts is difficult, but it offers interesting possibilities for integration.

Socio-cultural Impacts on Tourism

Tourism has clear socio-cultural implications. It affects tourists, hosts and host-guest relationships. The impacts on hosts that Mathieson and Wall refer to can to a large extent be classified as economic. For socio-cultural impacts to occur, some form of contact between hosts and guests has to be established. According to De Kadt there are three types of such contact. Contact occurs:

— when tourists buy goods and services

— when hosts and tourists share a facility

— when tourists and hosts meet for cultural exchange

Apart from these more or less formalized forms of contact, interaction may also occur through the mere physical presence of tourists. According to UNESCO host-guest relationships, especially in the case of mass tourism, are characterised by four special features:

1. Their transitory nature
2. *Temporal and spatial constraints*: Tourists are often separated physically from the local population, which reduces the possibilities of contact. Also, tourists attempt to see and do as much as possible in the relatively short time available. This hinders contact.
3. *Lack of spontaneity*: Formerly informal human interaction such as hospitality are drawn into the area of economic activity, formalising relationships to a large extent.
4. *Unequal and unbalanced experiences*: Material inequality often exists and is seen in tourist spending and attitudes. Hosts often feel inferior and, to compensate for this, exploit the tourists' apparent wealth.

Actual impacts depend upon three major aspects:

1. Cultural and economic distances between tourists and hosts In general, the greater these distances the greater the impact. If a tourist is not aware of certain values in the destination, he runs a high risk of violating them. On the other hand, if a host is not

aware of the fact that many tourists need to work all year to be able to afford their holidays, feelings of envy are bound to be stronger.

2. *Absorption capability*: Problems are bound to arise once more tourists arrive than a destination's facilities can sustain. In such cases direct competition arises between tourists and the host population.
3. *Pace of tourism development*: Development which is too rapid leads to overdependency on tourism and to serious social adjustment problems.

In short, a thousand Dutch tourists probably have a greater socio-cultural effect on a small but rapidly developing destination in Africa than on a well-established destination such as Paris. In the literature about socio-cultural impacts a distinction is often made between social and cultural aspects. The social aspects cover interpersonal relations, whereas the cultural aspects consider both material and non-material forms of culture.

Many possible social impacts of tourism have been put forward in the literature, most of which are negative. Not every form of socio-cultural change is necessarily bad, however. In order to reach a higher standard of living, some socio-cultural changes are often needed. But this does not need to damage social or cultural identity.

Unfortunately, no generally accepted classification of social impacts seems to exist in the literature. The existing classifications lack a logical structure and their impact categories are overlapping. Especially young people tend to imitate the tourists' behaviour. They are attracted by the tourists' clothing and eating habits and their spending patterns. This is called the demonstration effect.

The problem is that the local population often cannot afford the tourists' behaviour, which may lead to feelings of frustration. Older people can also become frustrated with tourism development. On the one hand they see the advantages of tourism in terms of employment and income, but on the other hand they see the disadvantages, for example in terms of loss of culture. This ambiguous attitude may produce feelings of resentment.

Population structure can be affected by tourism. First of all, by strengthening the economic basis of the local community, tourism may foster population growth. This population growth often comes about by immigration. People from other areas are lured to the tourist destination by the possibility of finding a better paid job. Movements of people appear to be both age- and sex-selective.

For example, according to Pearce, people aged twenty to thirty and females are overrepresented in the tourist destination of Queenstown, New Zealand. One of the main characteristics of tourism is its seasonal nature. During the high season, employment opportunities are far greater than during the low season. This is often reflected in population structures.

Workers flow in and out of the destination together with the tourists. This makes it hard for the local population to develop a sense of community. Moreover, the seasonal workers do sometimes not belong to the same culture as the autochthonous population. Tourism offers new employment opportunities, which may draw workers from other sectors of the economy - for example, agriculture - with consequent effects on class or social structure. Also, activities may become financially rewarded, which were not paid for in earlier times.

Tourism can place people, especially women and young people, in a financially less dependent position. This can drastically alter hierarchical structures in society. By using facilities and resources in the destination, tourists can have a serious impact on daily life. Tourism may for example lead to water shortages as aggregate demand for water is greater than supply. This phenomenon may be worsened by the earlier discussed demographic processes.

According to Figuerola values in society can be grouped into four categories: political, social, religious and moral. The transformation of values is related to the demonstration effect, which occurs when different groups of people are brought together. Lambiri-Dimaki notes the democratisation and modernisation of attitudes amongst the young, arising out of contact with youthful Western tourists. Often negative developments of moral behaviour are attributed to tourism.

Such developments include prostitution, gambling and crime. It is hard to determine the exact role of tourism in these developments. All of them are present in almost every society, with or without tourism. However, tourism may have created locations and environments which prostitution, gambling and crime need to flourish. In the case of prostitution, Mathieson and Wall mention, among others, the following hypothetical processes:

— Tourism means that people are away from the puritanical bonds of normal living and money is available to spend hedonistically.

— Tourism affords employment for women, so it may upgrade their economic status.

This, in turn, may lead to their liberalisation and, eventually, to their involvement in prostitution to maintain or acquire new economic levels. The latter hypothesis is of course closely related to earlier comments on the transformation of forms and types of employment.

Contact between hosts and tourists may give rise to changed consumption patterns. This may be due to the demonstration effect or to increased income levels. If a tourist is rich and successful in the eyes of the host, the latter may try to emulate the formers behaviour and consumption pattern. In the process the host may forget that the tourist often seems better off than he really is. After all, tourism is a hedonistic experience which most tourists cannot afford on a sustained basis.

The significance of the demonstration effect for changing consumption patterns probably increases with increasing cultural and economic distances. Tourism may indirectly change consumption patterns by increasing abilities. A higher income level means more consumption possibilities.

Tourism may give rise to health problems in at least two ways. First of all, by moving around the world tourists may spread diseases such as AIDS, cholera or malaria. Second, the movement of tourists or of people employed in the tourism industry may lead to excessive use of facilities such as sewage treatment which may present health risks.

Tourism is sometimes accused of being a neo-colonialist industry. It is directed from the large metropolitan areas in the Western world, leaving the rest of the world without much control and in a dependent situation. Neo-colonialism can give local people a feeling of frustration and inferiority. Once large multinational corporations gain control in a destination, a large part of tourist expenditure ends up in the Western home countries of those corporations.

Another expression of neo-colonialism may be the intensification of racial or ethnic differences. Tourism is highly related to the service sector. Therefore one could argue that the local population is serving the (Western) tourist, just like in the colonial times. It is feared that this undermines the local population's self respect. However, service is not the same as servility. People can work in the service industry without losing their self esteem.

Many possible and actual social impacts can be summed up, but unfortunately not many frameworks are available to assess them in a coherent way. Mathieson and Wall mention two such frameworks. In a sense these frameworks offer a possibility to assess perceptions by locals of tourism development. The first one is the irritation index of Doxey, which describes a transitory development of host attitudes through five stages:

— *level of euphoria*: locals err enthusiastic and thrilled by tourist development

— *level of apathy*: tourists become targets for profit-taking

— *level of irritation*: locals cannot handle the large number of tourists

— *level of antagonism*: tourism is a scapegoat for all that is bad

— *final level*: locals must learn to live in an altered environment

A probably more realistic approach is taken by Bjorklund and Philbrick. Here, the host population is not seen as a homogeneous group, but as made up of individuals with varying interests and other characteristics. In the Bjorklund-Philbrick framework, four responses to tourism development are identified, ranging from aggressive promotion to silent opposition.

People's responses are dependent on the distribution of advantages and disadvantages from tourism development. Entrepreneurs making a profit out of tourism and not bearing a significant part of the costs associated with it, can be expected to be aggressive promoters. On the other hand, fishermen seeing their fishing grounds become polluted and less accessible will be aggressive opponents.

People's place in the matrix may change, however, in any direction. Fishermen, for example, may find a job as a tourist guide. Then, costs and benefits to them are more equilibrated, possibly leading to a response shift towards slight support of tourism development.

Culture can be divided into material and non-material elements. In turn, non-material culture can be divided into habits and customs and non-material art forms. The forms of material culture which are most important for tourism are handicrafts and architecture. Tourism often leads to the commercialisation of art forms and especially handicrafts.

Artefacts with cultural or religious meaning are sought by tourists as souvenirs. As more and more tourists visit a destination, souvenir production is increased, often leading to mass production. In the process, the cultural artefacts may lose their cultural meaning. On the other hand, tourism may also stimulate a renewed attention for old cultural traditions and art forms, often combined with insights from other parts of the world.

According to Mathieson and Wall this has been the case in the United States where Pueblo Indians combined Indian and Western techniques to create new forms of art. This development could not have taken place without the financial stimulus of tourism. Impacts on architecture, which is another form of material culture, are of another nature. These arise mostly because tourist buildings are not built according to local architectural standards. To give an example, whereas in many less developed countries high-rise buildings are rare, hotels are often many stories high.

Impacts on non-material culture, such as dance or religious manifestations, are similar to impacts on material art forms. Here too, cultural expressions may lose their deeper significance when confronted with commercialisation. But tourism may also give rise to a revival of old art forms, perhaps mixed with influences from other cultures.

Commercially produced art forms without significance, also called fake art or airport art, may be used to distract tourist attention from the real cultural expressions by the local population. In general, tourists are looking for "typical" forms of local culture. These can be offered to them in the form of typical souvenirs or exhibitions of the local way of life in specially designed imitation villages.

In such settings, visual or audible art forms, such as local dances or songs can be performed. At the same time, locals can enjoy their own cultural manifestations, which may be less typical in they eyes of the tourist but more authentic and contemporary.

Two theories are available to describe tourism's impacts on habits and customs: acculturation theory and cultural shift theory. According to the acculturation theory cultural changes brought about by tourism are permanent. This theory states that when a strong and a weak culture meet, the weak culture adopts the habits and customs of the stronger culture.

A competing view is that hosts indeed change their behaviour when interacting with guests, but that these changes are only temporary and context-dependent. This is called cultural shift. Here, the changes are merely cosmetic instead of fundamental as in the case of acculturation. However, when cultural shift occurs over long periods of time, it may become more and more institutionalised, beginning to form part of local culture. In this way, cosmetic change may give rise to fundamental cultural change.

Tourist numbers are highest in the stagnation stage, although growth rates are low. In this stage massive numbers of tourists come on fully standardised packages and they expect Western amenities. To be able to offer these, a destination often separates tourist resorts from the local population. For the tourists, a so called "environmental bubble" is created in which the tourists can feel at home and safe. However, this separation may have serious consequences for the host population. Often, for example, use of beaches is restricted to tourists.

Contact between hosts and tourists is highly institutionalised. Hosts and tourists only meet at scheduled moments along the itinerary which the tour operator has planned. The increasing distance between tourists and the host population may give rise to the formation of caricaturistic images of each other. The characteristics of Doxey's stage of antagonism may apply, in which irritations become more overt and the tourist is seen as the harbinger of all that is bad.

The economic benefits may significantly decrease. On the one hand, initial expenditure -at least per tourist - can be expected to decrease due to bargaining by the tour operators. On the other hand, leakages are expected to increase. Control is now firm in the hands of foreigners, who tend to repatriate important shares of their profits and wages. After the stagnation stage the succession of tourist types, from drifter to organised mass tourist, has come to an end. Often, this means that tourists and the tourism industry lose interest in the destination.

As growth comes to a standstill, so does investment. Now several scenario's can be imagined, such as decline and rejuvenation. In the decline scenario, the destination does not succeed in changing its image. Tourist numbers will decrease and investors move on, using the destination as a cash-cow. They try to squeeze as much money out of it without investing in improvement.

So, in economic terms, benefits from tourism are gradually declining. People realise that their culture and the environment have changed irreversibly and that it is too late to do something about it. Doxey's so-called final level of tourist irritation may apply in such a case. Another possible scenario is rejuvenation in which the destination tries to reposition itself in the tourism market.

A destination may for example decide to offer more possibilities for an active vacation, whereas the focus used to be on quite passive vacations by the elderly. The destination life cycle is a useful concept for the description of possible forms and consequences of tourism development. It focuses attention on some important mechanisms of tourism development. However, the destination life cycle should not be looked upon as a inevitable process.

An important contribution of the life cycle concept is its focus on both temporal and physical concentration. The first is related to growth rates, the second to absolute numbers in relation to the destination's resources. Both types of concentration can be analysed in terms of carrying capacity. In the context of tourism, the concept of carrying capacity can be defined as the maximum number of people who can use a site without an unacceptable alteration in the human and natural environment and without an unacceptable decline in the quality of the experience gained by visitors.

The concept of carrying capacity is used mostly when assessing the environmental impacts of tourism. However, the concept is also applicable to other impacts such as socio-cultural and economic ones. According to Müller five important dimensions of tourism development exist, together forming the "magic pentagon".

Economic health, well-being of locals, protection of resources and a healthy culture assume respect for the economic, social, environmental and cultural carrying capacities respectively. Maybe satisfaction of guests can also be described in such terms: a "satisfactional" carrying capacity. According to Müller sustainable tourism can only exist if none of the mentioned carrying capacities are violated. In practice, however, there appears to be a trade-off between the short term need for economic development and the long term sustainability interests.

In short, the development of tourism is closely linked to macro-level economic, technological, demographic and institutional developments. In the post-war period, economic and technological developments have been enormous, while popuiation growth has slowed down. This, together with institutional developments like the introduction of holiday allowances, have led to rapid tourism development.

3

Tourism Liberalisation

Tourism is one of the oldest areas of economic activity to be covered under the WTO's General Agreement on Trade in Services (GATS). Tourism and travel related services account for about 11% of World GDP and employ about 200 million people worldwide. They also represent 34% of world service exports.

Furthermore, given that there are about 700 million international travellers per year, tourism and travel related sectors have become dynamic sources of income and a major strategic sector for development in many countries, especially those in the global South. Tourism and travel related services are still strongly dominated by Northern countries.

The main sources remain Europe and the US, with some new influx form Asia and Latin America. Almost half of world tourists come from six countries in Europe which are also among the world's top ten tourism earners/spenders). The US is number one in tourism spending/earning and the second most popular destination. East Asia and the Pacific are expected to be second in generating tourists in 2020.

The rise in technology, which is critical for success in the tourism and travel sectors, advantages the North, allowing for further consolidating of their stronghold over this sector. The control of core tools of tourism is found in the North: air travel, hotel, Internet and e-commerce. Increasingly electronic technology is facilitating the sale and marketing of airline tickets and hotel accommodations.

This is an important context from which to consider the likely consequences of the growing push for greater and rapid liberalisation in tourism by the North. Because the central tendency of liberalization is to reduce the role of developing country governments in directing tourism investment and policies, serious questions exist as to the future of tourism as a tool for development in the South.

Modern international tourism is rooted in the dynamics of colonialism and dependency. As Chachage, Munt and Naipaul noted, early nineteenth century tourism focused on exploration, hunting and trading in colonial territories. This was a fact of colonial conquest and hence was linked to the issues of the alienation from land and natural resources with underlying ethnic racial, class and gender dynamics.

This form of tourism and its gains were controlled by the colonial power, tour operators and owners of steamships and domestic railroads within the countries. This tourism was also primarily extractive and depleted natural resources such as skins, ivory and fauna, in order to sustain the wealthy.

The development of mass tourism in the 1950s and 60's led to the inclusion of the middle class in "fun and sun" adventures in the developing world. But even the new forms of tourism of the 1980's and 1990s still carry echoes of the past as it is increasingly returning to the theme of exploiting the "exotic" and nature.

Today the mechanism and devices of control and access to tourist arrivals and the struggle between sending and host countries over retention of tourist expenditures are different. But developing countries still have weak bargaining power vis-à-vis international tour operators and experience discrimination.

Ultimately, these countries must survive in an increasingly competitive global tourism sector in which natural competitive advantage is becoming less and less significant. Tourism is more than ever an information sensitive industry which is greatly impacted by modern technological innovations such as the Internet, worldwide web and electronic commerce. Unfortunately, these tend to widen the divide between developed and developing countries with the potential for siphoning much of the potential gains from tourism back to the developed countries.

There is growing consolidation and centralization of the tools of the tourism trade among a few players. These players, who are primarily based in the North, control the information and online reservation services. New information technology and networks such as the Internet therefore have an important affect on the trade competitiveness of developing countries.

The development and interlink of tourism and e-commerce is resulting in the slow demise of travel agents; increasing resort to proprietary web pages; on-line one stop shopping; and a more complex tourism product-which involves the consumer being able to customise her/his itinerary. But many travel agents in developing countries do not have access to the investment capital to participate effectively with foreign tourism suppliers.

The biggest myth of tourism and development is that 'tourism is quick, cheap and easy, given that the basic ingredients are sun, sea, smile and culture'. In its most basic form tourism builds on nature, adventure and culture. Tourism is expected to generate revenue in the form of foreign exchange earnings, increased income, employment and development of infrastructure-all this is expected to arise from the net benefit of tourism receipts.

Ultimately, tourism should also generate demand from other sectors of the economy such as agriculture, manufacturing and other services. Growth in tourism is also argued to facilities foreign capital inflows which reduce the need for domestic savings and capital accumulation. Tourism can be good for development when it engenders a strong inflow of foreign exchange, and positive intersectoral linkages, which promote growth of other sectors. This increases overall income and employment in the economy.

Tourism can also lead to immiserating growth (there is some growth but it is accompanied by rising poverty and unemployment) if the output of non-traded goods and services the tourism sector requires does not increase. Thus the conventional wisdom that tourism is unambiguously good is problematic.

— First, it does not recognise the drain of resources and loss of revenues abroad.

— Second, it often ignores distributional and other key factors associated with the goods and services used by the tourists.

— Third, it ignores the social, gender equity and environment impacts of the welfare effects of tourism.

The trend towards more and more privatisation and liberalisation may in fact dissipate the benefits of tourism on development in spite of the widely acknowledged increasing demand for certain types of leisure activities and the availability of abundant female labour. Thus tourism development may not be in line with social, sustainable development for some of these reasons:

—Ownership of resources, which is skewed to the North and Northern based foreign direct investment.

—Most small and medium sized businesses, which are the major local players in developing countries, cannot compete with the large well financed and overly capital endowed foreign competitors.

—Problems around land (land grabbing and land speculation. The rapid expansion of tourism is encouraged by the privatization of government owned assets including parks, and community lands that have traditionally been the homes and sources of livelihood for many citizens for generations. Privatization and land speculation to establish game reserves or other tourist attractions creates greater inequality in access to common property resources and raises the price of existing real estate. In the worst case it may be associated with large-scale removal of entire groups of people. All of these have the impact of exacerbating poverty and crime and ultimately destabilizing the society.

— Ecological/environmental effects.

— Gender bias and inequities: trafficking, sex tours: women's health and morbidity

— Poverty and inequality.

— Displacement of other sectors, such as decline in domestic agricultural sector.

The issue of tourism, tourism development and gender equality is multi-dimensional. It ranges from the low profile and persistent issue of the lopsided responsibility for social reproduction and community resource management between men and women; the differential and gender-based nature and consequences of access to social and economic resources; the pervasive reliance on (and at the same time the invisibility of) women's labour in the hospitality sector; and the high profile issues of sex tourism and HIV/AIDS.

All women from peasant women, indigenous women, working women, old women, young women and girls, and women who head household are affected to different degree by tourism and tourism development. Men of different social classes are also affected negatively and positively by changes in the tourism sector. And men in poorer classes may also suffer similarly to poor women from the welfare reducing impact of loss of access to resources.

Undeniably, there are significant gender biases and inequality in terms of access to employment and physical and social resources that may predispose women to have greater vulnerabilities and constraints in enjoying the presumed benefits of tourism development. We can demarcate these impacts across four categories:

1) Employment in the formal labour market,
2) Women's activities in the informal sectors and sustainable livelihood,

3) Women's social economic empowerment (in terms of consumption and access to resources including government services and

4) Women's influence and decision-making around tourism development policy.

Like all other forms of employment, access to tourism-related employment is gender based. Men tend to predominate in the formal sector of the tourism in some countries in the South. In India, women equal a small percentage of the employed (2.98%), and in Sri Lanka it is higher. In the Caribbean and Latin America the percentage is significantly higher at 35%. Men and women, who are seen as cheaper labour than men, are segregated due to gender stereotyping and sex segregation into different occupations.

Even where women are the main tourism workers, they tend to predominate in the majority of menial, semi-skilled, domestic and service type occupations. For example in Barbados and Jamaica, women are employed in less stable, lower status work such as housekeeping, reception and other services. Due to lack of unionization, these jobs require low skill, are low paid and have the lowest security of tenure and benefits.

In some countries men are often employed as stewards, porters, and tend to be over-represented in professional managerial and supervisory positions. A recent survey of the literature on women and tourism by Equations points out the following:

In the food sector of the industry women are at the bottom of the hierarchy as restaurant helpers, cooks (not Chefs) and waitresses-all the lowest paid parts of the food sectors. Chefs in fancier restaurants where salaries and tips are substantial are more likely to be males.

In the travel sector, women have access and employment to seasonal, part-time or minimum wage jobs. Women tend to dominate small travel agencies and the majority are travel agents but men control the major sectors: airlines, railroads, hotel chains, car rental companies, travel magazines. Foreign control areas are also male dominated. The sexual division of labour operates at all aspects of tourism and travel related industries.

Given the condition of work, generally low pay, lack of benefits and absence of human resource development in this area, serious concerns arise about women's longer-term prosperity. Though increased tourism may mean more jobs for women questions must be raised about the nature, quality and type of work activities available; and the differential access of men and women to such opportunities.

In addition, there is the larger picture of tourism relation to women's longer term interests and its potential for the transformation of gender inequalities and biases. In the informal sector gender hierarchies also exist. Women dominate in the informal sectors where they provide a wide range of services to tourists-washing clothes, petty trading, cooking and childcare.

The Equation survey and Badger 1993 report point to the fact that there are 'gender differences in the selling of memories'. Women are often involved in the production of ethnic handicrafts and the marketing of such items while men provide services and support women's home craft production. In some cases while women produce the works and sell them in local markets, men control the wholesaling in urban centres. Overall, some women in some countries may gain financial autonomy and some measure of economic independence from their participation in informal markets linked to the tourism trade.

Sex tourism

Women are often exploited in the marketing of tourism (given existing gender perceptions and stereotypes that dominates social relations in the host and sending countries). As seen above, even in the formal labour markets there is the manipulation of the sexual division of labour that shunts women to the lowest paid jobs. Likewise, as noted by Badger there is much manipulation of gender differences in order to 'feed the fantasy of the male tourist'.

Very often this occurs at the benign level of women being offered opportunities in frontline (hospitality) positions in the tourism industry. Such opportunities are linked to women's presumed feminine qualities of being more sociable and more hospitable than men. But increasingly women are directly exploited as sexual playthings and earners of foreign exchange in prostitution (a traditional activity) and now the new explosion of sex tourism.

As noted by Badger 'sex tourism is now becoming one of the 'steadiest, least seasonal and most lucrative opportunities for women'. The down side is that it has tremendous health hazards and it can be dangerous. The issue of sex tourism has been raised as a key issue in the appeal of ASEAN (Association of Southeast Asian Nations) destinations.

This is particularly the case in Thailand and Cambodia where there is an influx of young girls who are from Burma, Indonesia, Laos and China who are being exported to work in Thai bars and brothels. In Cambodia, children are often bought and sold like cattle in Bangkok or the beach resorts and there is an active slave trade in young sex workers. Vulnerable women and children are preyed upon and girls 13-17 are forced into sex work; many start as housekeepers and then go to Karaoke bars or nightclubs.

The pervasiveness of sex tourism in Thailand has led to it being referred as 'Thighlandia'. This trend does not only apply to South Asia. Sex tourism is an enduring feature of Caribbean tourism. While in some cases such as the gay and paedophilia market the customers are exclusively male, this is not true for the Caribbean where there is high incidence of female customers patronising male sex suppliers.

Women's social and economic status and overall economic empowerment are influenced by their status and role in the family and community; their social reproduction responsibilities (as purveyors of food and essential services) and their access, ownership and control over their resources. Tourism impacts greatly on all of these, negatively or positively.

In terms of family and community life, tourism can either bring greater access to basic services (road, water, electricity and sanitation) or it may reduce such access if services are diverted to hotels and resorts or there are restrictions on access to local resources due to tourism development. For example, it is reported that in Western Samoa, tourism has led to the commoditization of traditional beliefs and practices and undermines traditional customs that gave specific well-defined rights and resources to men and women.

Through its direct impact on local prices (land and food) as well as its indirect impact via changes in the exchange rate, tourism can add to women's social reproduction burden. It certainly will impact their access to and ownership of economic resources. Furthermore, if tourism development is promoted via tax breaks for hotels and the construction of tourist attractions, this will divert resources from the social budget with negative implications for social services.

All of these have negative impacts on women's daily lives, work activities, food & nutritional status, and access to education and health care. Thus as Fillmore argues, women often pay the cost of tourism disproportionately while reaping few of the benefits. On the positive side, increased employment in tourism can increase women's financial and economic autonomy.

Likewise, increased revenue from the tourist sector into the government coffers may be available for the promotion of social development. Thus much depends on the governments' ability and willingness to use fiscal and monetary measures to ensure that there is social development linked to increased tourism development. Governments would also have to take proactive measure to promote better jobs and working conditions at all levels of the tourism sector as well as special policies to promote women's involvement at the higher and more lucrative levels of the tourism sector.

Whether such actions are possible and chosen by economic decision-makers will depend on two main factors: the opportunities and constraints built into the multilateral trading system which now governs tourism and the activism of women and other social activists to create governments that work in the interest of gender equity and human development.

In general, the political and economic forums that structure and drive tourism policy and tourism development are dominated by male economic agents. Few women get to play an active role in shaping tourism policy and practise at an official level. But increasingly, women in their many roles are finding ways to have an active voice in tourism.

The struggle over the nature, extent and pace of further liberalization in this sector and other sectors is now ongoing over the liberalization agenda of the World Trade Organization. This arena provides a good space for women's activism on these issues locally, nationally, regionally and globally.

Thus defined, international tourism is increasingly becoming a significant part of global trade. It is one of the top five export categories for about 83% of countries in the world. International trade in tourism is concentrated in developed countries. The share of the South is about 1/3 of total international tourism. But it is a fundamental source of income and foreign exchanges for a number of Southern countries.

Tourism is lauded for having a higher positive multiplier spillover effect than most economic sectors. It is widely claimed that for each job created in tourism there are 9 jobs generated in other areas. To date it is the only sector in the service area where developing countries have consistent surpluses.

East Asia and the Pacific are the fastest growing tourism areas, but there is a high degree of concentration of arrivals and receipts among and within the South. Singapore, Hong Kong and China each have a higher sum of tourist arrivals and receipts than the sum of Thailand, Indonesia and South Asia.

Tourism is also linked to other areas of the economy: agriculture, land and labour. It is also inextricably intertwined with air transportation, the major means used by tourists arriving in the South, and communication. Given this, the liberalisation of tourism has major implications for social development and gender equality.

Liberalization tends to 'prioritize global commerce over everything: self-reliance of communities, human rights and health and safety' (Pera and McLaren, 1998). Andrea Yoder writes that there is already a problem in enforcing standards in the tourism industry such as prior informed consent for local initiatives, and environmental regulations.

Many of these pro-social and human development measures are already in conflict with WTO rules. Wallach and Sforza write that WTO orchestrated uniform global standards [which are designed by TNCs] to promote harmonisation of standards may 'facilitate the growth of consumer culture, [but they] militate against standards which reflect differences in cultural values. Such differences are seen as undesirable because they fragment the global market'. In this context a great deal of attention and importance must be focused on the current negotiations for further liberalization of tourism under the GATS. The direct impacts of the GATS as it relates to tourism would include:

— The GATS would allow foreign companies to merge or take over local companies. This is a threat to indigenous-owned and operated sustainable tourism initiatives.

— The GATS would allow upward pressure on the exchange rates with implications for real wages, price of land and other resources as well as for traditional exports such as agriculture, mining and fishing.

— Domestic regulation rules may impact governments' use of taxation policies to prevent de-industrialisation and de-agriculturalization.

— Governments will not be able to mitigate or limit the impact of the outflow of repatriated earnings from FDI, which will result in reduced welfare.

— GATS may also prove detrimental to eco and heritage tourism development.

— The GATS also has serious implication for pro-poor tourism that attempts to generate net benefits to the poor. The core of this strategy is to 'unlock opportunities for the poor with tourism rather than to expand the overall size of the sectors. But this requires domestic regulation to remove some barriers to entry and to enhance their ability to participate effectively in tourism.

The idea that tourism will yield overwhelmingly positive benefits on growth on development. But this is based on input / output studies that show that increased tourism implies across the board expansion of economic activity. This ignores distributional impacts and forward and backward linkages that are endemic problems in developing countries' economies.

It also does not take into account that tourism growth may come with increased competition with other sectors such as domestic agriculture and other export areas. Most of these sectors are the ones which provide wages for women. And, while tourism may bring employment it is often seasonal and highly exploitative.

It also points to some strategic interventions that are important for a promoting more balanced gender and social equity outcomes of GATS driven liberalization of tourism services. However, the strategic interventions dedicated to promoting the long-term strategic gender interest of women are predicated on a certain amount of latitude in developing countries ability to manipulate and regulate the agents, mechanisms and processes of tourism development.

Trends in Tourism

Recent shifts in world tourism, partly resulting from the 11 September terrorist attacks in the United States, provide an incentive to take stock of the Antarctic tourism industry and look at likely future directions.

Commercial Antarctic tourism probably started in the mid-1950s when a Chilean national airline carried 66 passengers aboard a Douglas DC6-B on an Antarctic overflight. In the late 1950s commercial ship tours from Chile and Argentina took passengers to the South Shetland Islands and the northwestern Antarctic Peninsula. Dedicated Antarctic ship-cruising began in the late-1960s when Lars-Eric Lindblad operated his purpose-designed Lindblad Explorer for nature-based, including Antarctic, cruising.

The number of tourists overflying and visiting the Antarctic and associated islands is very small compared with most other tourist destinations and activities, but these numbers and the range of activities are slowly growing -roughly doubling over the past decade. This is largely a result of ice-class vessels from the former Soviet Union becoming available for charter during the 1990s for tourist cruises.

Information from the International Association of Antarctica Tour Operators (IAATO) indicates the total number of tourists visiting and overflying Antarctica in the 2000 -01 Antarctic summer season was about 2000 fewer than in the previous season. This is thought to be due to the unusually high number of tourism activities throughout the world during the millennium year and to the unavailability last summer of three cruise vessels that had operated in the 1999 -2000 season.

IAATO estimated at the 2001 Antarctic Treaty Consultative meeting that numbers for 2001 -02 would be over 20,000, including 14,500 from cruise ships and land-based activities (some air-supported), 2,400 on large cruise vessels that did not involve landings, and 3,585 undertaking overflights or landing briefly.

Before the 11 September attacks, tourist numbers were predicted to rise to over 34,000 by 2005 -06, much of that coming from non-landing passengers on large tourist vessels. There may be fewer US nationals travelling and reduced early-season numbers. The predicted increase in Antarctic tourist numbers may well eventuate, with three tour companies proposing to operate four large passenger vessels in the Peninsula area in the coming season.

Operators of large passenger vessels have previously been excluded from IAATO membership, but at its 2001 meeting the Association agreed to create a new membership category for companies with vessels able to carry more than 500 passengers, subject to those vessels not landing passengers in Antarctica.

The overwhelming majority of Antarctic tourism is in the Antarctic Peninsula area, south of South America, and associated subantarctic islands, and most tours operate out of either Ushuaia (Argentina), Punta Arenas

(Chile), or Stanley (Falkland Islands). Landings in the Ross Sea area, southeast of Australia, currently comprise only about three percent of all tourist landings in Antarctica.

Australia's involvement in commercial Antarctic tourism is multifaceted, involving cruise operations out of Hobart to the Ross Sea region, Commonwealth Bay and the Australian and New Zealand subantarctic islands; Antarctic overflights; and Australian companies (currently five) operating cruise and adventure tours in the Antarctic Peninsula area. In 2002 -03, Albany in Western Australia will be the finishing point for a proposed tourist cruise to subantarctic islands in the southern Indian Ocean, including Kerguelen and Heard Islands.

Between November to February each summer, over 2,000 passengers experience Antarctica via overflights from Sydney or Melbourne, or occasionally Adelaide or Perth. Chartering Qantas 747-400 aircraft, the Melbourne company Croydon Travel organises around six flights a season, each lasting around 12 hours. A highlight in past sea-Global and regional climate change and managing the Southern Ocean ecosystem are the main study themes among the 54 Antarctic research projects granted Australian Government funding totalling $670,000 for 2002 -03.

Announcing the Australian Antarctic Science (AAS) grants, Dr Sharman Stone, Parliamentary Secretary responsible for the Antarctic, said the scheme illustrated the Government's commitment to supporting long-term Antarctic research, both for understanding regional and global processes and for helping to preserve the region's natural qualities.

'Australia leads the world in research into managing Southern Ocean fisheries, covering development of a sustainable fishery and the conservation of animals - notably seabirds -endangered by that activity. Dr Stone said.. The Australian Antarctic Division's Chief Scientist, Prof. Michael Stoddart, said that with the Australian research program's five-year science plan now three years old, a more complete picture of fundamental processes and changes in the region was beginning to emerge. Among projects supported this season are:

— an intensive Australian-German study of the physical and climatic history of Antarctica's remote southern Prince Charles Mountains, seeking to fill major gaps in knowledge of a period when Australia and Antarctica were one continent;

— a study of the production and movement of extremely cold, dense 'Antarctic Bottom Water 'to improve climate forecasting models and understanding of their influence on Southern Ocean ecosystems;

— analysis of contaminated sites in Antarctica to guide work to manage the contaminants and rehabilitate the sites producing new technology with application to similar sites elsewhere in the world;

— studies of fur seals on Australia's subantarctic islands which have indicated rapidly rising numbers with implications for Southern Ocean fisheries;

— investigations of the upper atmosphere above Antarctica and near-Earth space to develop our understanding of the role and influence of this coldest part of the Earth's atmosphere on weather and climate throughout the world; and

— use of robot technology to investigate growth patterns of microscopic plants that grow on the underside of sea ice off the coast of Antarctica.

Like all tourists, visitors to Antarctica are constantly seeking new experiences, reflected in the changing range of tour activities and destinations. Mountain climbing, snow-boarding and kayaking are regular highlights on some tours, but recent and proposed activities include half and full marathons run at the South Pole, a circumnavigation of Antarctica, a North Pole -South Pole overflight, and an overflight tracking progress of a total solar eclipse over Dronning Maud and Queen Mary Lands in November 2003.

The future also may see a push for greater involvement of aircraft to transport tourists to Antarctica. Over the past decade, US-based Adventure Network International has provided air transport and ground support for trekking, climbing and other adventure activities on the continent, mainly from ANI's summer base camp in the Patriot Hills, Ellsworth Land. Flights to the continent are also provided by Chilean companies, and 2001 -02 saw the establishment of a company offering tourist flights from Cape Town to Dronning Maud Land, although no tourists were actually carried this season.

4

Market Research in Travel and Tourism

Tourism is getting more and more important. Despite the fear of terrorism, the market of tourism is growing steadily the last few decades. Not only on a global scale, but also on a national scale. For example the Netherlands. The total tourism within the Netherlands is increasing. Not only the Dutch make more trips and spent more time on tourism and leisure, foreigners also visited the Netherlands more often.

According to the WTO/United Nations Recommendations on Tourism Statistics,' Tourism comprises the activities of persons travelling to and staying in places outside their usual environment for not more than one consecutive year for leisure, business and other purposes.' The use of this broad concept makes it possible to identify tourism between countries as well as tourism within a country.

Tourism refers to all activities of visitors, including both ' tourists' (overnight visitors) and ' same-day visitors'. It is an activity which has grown substantially over the last quarter of this century as an economic and social phenomenon. Tourism is by nature a demand phenomenon. Visitor consumption is the basic component of the demand approach.

Tourism demand does not correspond only to visitor consumption. It must also include other concepts related to the attention to visitors in a country of reference, without which tourism activity could hardly take place. More specifically:

— the existence of a basic infrastructure in terms of transport, accommodation, recreation, etc.;

— the role played by governments, at different levels, concerning the regulation of different activities associated to the development of tourism.

The term ' tourist' or ' visitor' describes ' any person travelling to a place other than that of his/her usual environment for less than 12 months and whose main purpose of visit is other than the exercise of an activity remunerated from within the place visited'. ' Traveller' refers to any person on a trip between two or more countries or between two or more localities within his/her country of usual residence.

Purpose of Tourism Statistics

For the purpose of tourism statistics and in conformity with the basic forms of tourism, visitors should be classified as:

International visitors

— Tourists (overnight visitors)

— Same-day visitors

Domestic visitors

— Tourists (overnight visitors)

— Same-day visitors.

The purpose of introducing the concept ' usual environment' is to exclude from the concept of ' visitor' persons travelling every day or week between their home and place of work or study, or other places frequently visited. The definition of usual environment is therefore based on the following criteria:

— Minimum distance travelled to consider a person a visitor;

— Minimum duration of absence from usual place of residence;

— Minimum change between localities or administrative territories.

The terms ' trip', ' visit' or ' journey' describe any travel to a place outside one's usual environment. And as you travel more than one day, you need a place to sleep. Tourism ' accommodation' refers to any facility that regularly provides overnight accommodation for tourists.

The following are the different types of tourism:

— *Domestic tourism*: is the tourism of resident visitors within the economic territory of the country of reference;

— *Inbound tourism*: is the tourism of non resident visitors within the economic territory of the country of reference;

— *Outbound tourism*: is the tourism of resident visitors outside the economic territory of the country of reference;

— *Internal tourism*: is the tourism of visitors, both resident and non resident, within the economic territory of the country of reference;

— *National tourism*: is the tourism of resident visitors, within and outside the economic territory of the country of reference.

Because tourism is a boundary crossing concept, it is somewhat difficult to segment the market and look at this market in a one simple straight way. So in my point of view there are two ways to look at tourism: take the country as object or take the people as objects. If we take the Netherlands for example again, you can look at tourism in Holland (internal tourism) and / or tourism by Dutch people (national tourism).

Tourism in Holland is made by Dutch tourists staying in their own country (domestic tourism) and by foreign people visiting Holland (inbound tourism). According to the data of the World Tourism Organization, international tourist arrivals amounted to 693 million in 2001, 4 million down from the 697 million of 2000 due to the weakening economies of major tourism generating markets and the impact of the terrorist attacks of September 11. Most affected regions were South Asia, the Americas and Middle East. Europe registered the same decrease as the world, and Africa and East Asia and the Pacific recorded positive percentages of 3.8 and 5.5 respectively.

A 463 billion US$ international tourism receipts were recorded worldwide in 2001. Tourists shifted their travel habits during this period of time, they chose closer and less expensive destinations. Half of the receipts were collected by Europe, and almost a third by the Americas

(26.4%), followed by East Asia and the Pacific (17.7%), Africa (2.5%), Middle East (2.4%) and the last in the list, South Asia with 1 per cent.

For the first time in history, the number of international tourist arrivals has exceeded the 700 million, and despite all the grim expectations and debates about the economic crisis and the fear of terrorism, the year ended with a 3.1 per cent increase. Tourism has once again proven its resilience.

In total, according to the preliminary data sent to the World Tourism Organization from official sources throughout the world, almost 715 million international tourist arrivals were registered last year. That is 22 million more than in 2001 or, compared with the ' millennium year' which many experts claim should be taken as the reference, almost 19 million more than in 2000.

France is still the most popular destination in the world. Last year 76 million people visited this country. Spain is second with 52 million tourists. Third are the United States with 45.million, followed by Italy with 39 million and China with 36 million. The average amount people spend on holiday has decreased and the duration of the visits has become shorter.

So tourism recovery is underway: fear is progressively fading away and business is gradually returning to normal although some destinations might be negatively influenced by the fact that operators have reduced capacity. Recovery is most visible in intraregional travel, and in the regions of the Pacific, Europe and Africa.

The number of foreign tourists who visited Holland in 2002 has increased by 3% to 9.8 million. The

Netherlands Board of Tourism (TRN) announced this on the base of figures of the first three quarters of 2002 by Statistics Netherlands (CBS). Because of the trend of ' trips not far away from home' Holland is being visited by people of surrounding countries. The Belgians (+ 14%) visited the Netherlands in 2002 mainly for a short but active holiday.

The number of Germans has increased by 5%. German tourists are by far the most important group of foreign visitors for the Netherlands with a share of 30%, despite the decrease in 2000 and 2001. The amount of Americans fell by 9%. Asia is rising with a growth of 13%, partly because of the horticulture exposition Floriade.

According to the Netherlands Board of Tourism it is too early to give a well-founded prognosis for 2003 in view of the economic situation and the situation in the Middle East. De World Tourism Organization (WTO) also announced that the growth in Western Europe was almost 2%. So relatively speaking Holland did a better job than the average of Western Europe.

In order to know more about the decisions people make related to their holidays, some research has been done by the partners involved in the Space Explorer project. Space Explorer is Europe's first interactive computerised travel planner for business and pleasure. Developed by a pan-European consortium of six organisations including the EC, it combines a database of travel information with a series of easy-to-use interface screens.

In the report of New Media Services six "trigger" types (selection criteria) for European holidays are given to identify factors and give a short and strong overview of the European market of holidays:

— Who trigger: Number, age and size of holida / party;
— What trigger: Activities and facilities;
— When trigger: Frequency, date and duration;
— Where trigger: Location, setting and accommodation;
— How trigger: Budget, transport and journey options;
— Why trigger: Reasons and motivations for going on holiday.

Changes to Europe' s population and social structures are taking place at a rapid pace, which will increasingly effect the demand for tourist services in the near and longterm future. For example, Europe will have to deal with an ageing population. Increased life expectancy and falling birth rates are resulting in an older population profile. Older people go on holiday less frequently than younger, but more of these ' active seniors' have a larger budget to spend and with an incredible amount of spare time this group becomes more and more interesting.

Another demographic factor is the rapid increase in the number of households, especially in north and western Europe. Of course there is a corresponding decrease in the average size of households. Smaller households are inclined towards taking more foreign holidays and more but shorter trips at home. Another trend is that consumer behaviour is increasingly driven by individualisation.

A number of related factors seem to be driving this trend. First, a greater range of requirements and expectations is leading to increasing fragmentation and diversity of travel products. Second, a client oriented approach is becoming more and more necessary. Third, there is a heightened interest in educational, cultural and activity holidays. Last, Holiday bookings are being made closer and closer to the date of departure. As a result of all these factors there is a decrease in the number of all-in ' package' holidays and a rapid increase in demand for tailored holidays, where customers can choose more and more between different elements of their holidays.

European Travel Monitor analysed destination and activity preferences of both German and French holiday-makers. The destination ' sun and beach' is still the strongest preference, both at German and French tourists. After that the activities ' city break' and ' touring' are the most wanted. ' Countyside recreation' is more popular with the French than with the Germans. Other activities mentioned in the research were ' winter snow' (wintersport), ' other sporting' and a last category ' other' to make the list complete.

People are more and more searching for individualised experiences, also named as ' special interest tourism'. Such travellers are more interested in enriching their lives with various experiences than in passive entertainment. They are looking for an interactive travel experience, with a high level of commitment, specified to a thorough treatment of the ' special interest' subject or the destination concerned.

Escaping their daily lives, people often are going for adventurous, challenging experiences, somewhat uncomfortable. So the number and diversity of holiday activities increases each year as the thirst for something different is satisfied by progressive tour organisers and promoters.

More time will be available for tourism and leisure. An ever shorting working week will result in more time for holidays, especially short breaks over extended weekends. Additional figures from the ANWB show that the average length of trips amongst Dutch tourists is getting shorter from 15.2 days in 1969 to 12.4 days in 1993. Across Europe, the months of May to October are still the most popular with 69% of all outbound trips made during these five months.

Timing of holidays is mainly determined by activity. For instance, people go on a ski holiday during the winter months and to the sun and beach in the summer. But a beginning trend is that people want to be able to do every activity at any time during the whole year. For example, more and more people are going for a beach holiday also in the winter months. Then they are looking for the sun in places far away from their home.

The majority of tourism within Europe is plainly internal with European residents accounting for 70% of arrivals. That means there is a strong preference for holidays within Europe by European inhabitants. One of the factors is probably the removal of barriers to ' foreign' travel within the EC. The further integration of EC travel infrastructure and improved ease of travel across former national borders (both practical and psychological) will result in greatly increased travel within the EC.

For example the opening of the Channel tunnel will make short breaks to/from Paris, Brussels, and London much more feasible. In 1993, German consumers accounted for 26% of all spending on travel and touring by Europeans, an estimated amount of more than $ 38 millions of US dollars. So tourism from Germany is very strong. Indeed the tourism flow from Germany is the largest flow within Europe, not very surprisingly as Germany is the biggest country of Europe with the most inhabitants.

France is now the world' s leading tourist destination in terms of international arrivals and second only to the USA in international tourist receipts. In 1998, air transport represented 43 per cent of the total and road transport 42 per cent. Rail transport accounts for 7 per cent and sea transport for 8 per cent. Over time a clear trend can be observed of a slow but steady increase of air transport at the expense of road transport.

In Europe the car is the predominant mode of transport. Perhaps ' motor vehicle' would be a better description to accommodate motor bikes, coaches, camper vans, trucks etc. The car is also increasingly popular as a means of holiday travel. The car gives tourists great freedom and a feeling of independency. Research suggested that more than 50% of all travel within. France by foreigners was by private car. Rail, coach and air were the other modes of transport in the same order of importance.

The distinction is becoming increasingly blurred. More business people try to mix business with pleasure in the notice that the journey will be largely funded by their employer anyhow. According to figures up to 1998, leisure, recreation and holidays still represent the main purpose of visit, accounting for 62 per cent. Business travel accounts for 18 per cent of the total, the remaining 20 per cent being represented by other motives, i.e. visiting friends and relatives, for religious purposes/ pilgrimages, for health treatment and other. In the last ten years especially, the share of this last category has been rising.

This pattern doubtless mirrors the aforementioned trend towards market diversification and the division of holidays, with people travelling for shorter periods of time and for different reasons. This increase has basically detracted from the share of total trips made for leisure, recreation and holiday purposes, the share ascribed to travel for business and professional purposes having remained relatively stable. The underlying motivations of leisure, recreation and holidays are also very important.

Yuan and McDonald conducted research among people from France, Germany, Great-Britain and Japan in order to find the motivations to go on holiday abroad. They used the concepts of ' push' and ' pull' factors. Push factors are the socio-psychological motivations of an individual to go travelling. Yuan and McDonald distinguish in order of importance: ' novelty', ' escape', ' prestige', 'enhancement of kinship relations' and ' relaxation/hobbies'. Pull factors are those factors, which attract the individual to choose for a certain destination at the moment that the decision to go on holiday has been taken.. They distinguish: ' budget' , ' culture and history', 'wilderness' , 'ease of travel' , 'cosmopolitan environment', ' facilities' and 'hunting'.

Fodness conducted an extensive research to recreational travel motives in the United States of America. Different tests resulted in a scale of five basic factors, generated by factor analysis. These are the following five factors together with comments, to which consumers refer:

Tourists from one country do not necessarily share the same motivations, influences or triggers of those from another country of course. There are rich and diverse cultural differences. For example, guidelines issued by the British Tourist Authority to UK hotels and organisers have shown the need to adapt their marketing to the country in which they are trying to sell their services.

Belgian visitors like golfing, walking and cycling when they visit the UK. Norwegians like canal cruising. Argentines want to watch rugby. Visitors from Hong Kong do not want to walk. They enjoy pageantry but do not like rain. And Israelian visitors to London likes to go to the theatre almost every night. One of the ' triggers' which will variate from country to country is price/ budget. This is caused by the different ways the travel indistry is set up and operates in each country.

Factors of tourism

The most important factors, influencing tourism, have been identified. In short, the main reasons for the tourism growth, is the economical growth and the trust people have in the economy. Other important factors are: the prices, the population (age, life cycle, level of education), the amount of spare time, the weather and other incentives, like publicity.

TNO is the Dutch organization for applied scientific research. TNO Inro is the institute for traffic and transport, logistics and spatial development. TNO Inro has been involved in the constructing of a model calculating the economic effects of tourism, called the TOUR-model. In the international literature on tourism, the following factors are mentioned:

- Attitudinal factors;
- Economic demand factors;
- affecting the supply of tourist facilities and services, and
- Restrictions on travel abroad or to particular areas.

— Attitudinal and economic demand factors are seen as the primary factors.

The supply and restricting factors are of secondary importance. Models of total amount of travel abroad tend to focus on economic factors and some general longterm attitudinal factors. The main impact of supply factors and travel restrictions is on the choice of destinations within these totals. The TOUR-model, which has been mentioned before, has a similar structure. The TOUR-model focuses on tourism in the Netherlands. Looking closer to the structure of the TOUR-model it is seen that two steps are distinguished to predict tourism:

1. prediction of the participation, and
2. prediction of the behaviour

The factors influencing these concepts are different. The tourist participation is mainly influenced by the economic situation, because going on a holiday or something is a luxury thing. The Netherlands had a rather large economic growth in the last years of the previous century with an average economic growth of about 3% a year.

In the Netherlands and for the Dutch people this growth resulted in an ongoing increase in tourism and leisure activities. The economic influence on tourism in the TOUR-model is specified into four variables:

— gross domestic product;

— personal income;

— percentage of unemployment, and

— percentage of elderly people (over 65)

To predict the participation in tourism of the Dutch people, the model uses the data source CVO, where the total number of tourists is available. For foreign tourist participation in the. Netherlands a forecast is made, using the economic information of foreign countries, especially the surrounding countries.

The analyses of tourism in the Netherlands showed that the number of foreigners coming to the Netherlands (inbound), the number of holidays of Dutch people in the Netherlands (domestic) and the number of holidays of the Dutch in foreign countries (outbound), increased. The explanation of this growth can also be made by using the TOUR-model. The TOUR-model has indicated in the past that these two factors are very important. A connection has been observed between this and the use of accomodation, mode of transport i.e. by Dutch tourists (domestic and outbound).

The type of household gives a good explanation of the behaviour in tourism. Smaller households tend to spend more time outdoors than bigger households do. The decrease in household sizes in the Netherlands may influence the total time spent on outdoor recreation activities. The age of a person influences its behaviour, so also its tourist behaviour. Within the TOUR-model age is considered an important factor for all kind of tourists.

The TOUR-model makes a difference between Dutch and foreign tourists concerning income. For foreign tourists income influences the participation. For Dutch tourists, income influences the budget available for holidays. Indirectly this influences the number of holidays, the distance, the mode of transport etc. For the behaviour of Dutch tourists, the number of working hours is an important factor. The influence of this factor is complex.

Unemployment in the Netherlands decreased strongly at the end of the nineties in the last century. This resulted in less time and more money for holidays, for the former unemployed. Another trend is the increase of the number of part-time jobs and the decrease of the number of working hours. More and more people exchange salary for time. In the Netherlands the percentage of part-time jobs is growing almost every year. Of the 29 OESO-countries, Holland is the country with the most part-time jobs. In 1998, part-time workers did 30% of all work.

A growth in part-time work results in two aspects. Some people will work less and will have additional spare time. Others, who did not use to work, start working. They have less spare time, but they will have extra money available to go on holiday. At the end the net effect will be an increase of tourism.

Higher education levels lead to more outdoor activities and more travelling. A general rise in the education level in the near future may lead to an increase in outdoor recreation activities.

Households with a car spend more time outdoors and abroad, spend more money, and of course make more kilometres travelling than households without a car, because with a car the mobility of a household increases strongly. With the increase in car ownership in the Netherlands it can be expected that more time will be spent on tourism and leisure activities.

Especially for the explanation of the behaviour of foreign tourists, the supply level in the Netherlands, compared to the supply level in other potential holiday destinations is very important. The supply level includes the price level, the supply of accommodations, attractions, transport modes etc. For Dutch tourists other personal characteristics are a better explanation than the supply.

The only exception for Dutch tourists is the ownership of specific goods. An owner of a boat in the Netherlands is more likely to stay in the Netherlands. Somebody with a second house abroad will more likely leave the Netherlands. The ownership of such goods does influence the domestic / outbound behaviour.

The behaviour of tourists travelling in a group is very different of the behaviour of people who come ' on there own' (not organised). For the attraction of tourists to the Netherlands, the way of travelling has to be taken into account also. In the TOUR-model the difference in behaviour coursed by this factor, is indicated.

The type of foreigners coming to the Netherlands differs between the seasons. So, the season is influencing inbound tourism. For Dutch tourists the weather is very important. If the weather is bad in the summer season, more people will decide to leave the country and look for the sun elsewhere. The weather influences the domestic / outbound tourism.

Economic importance of tourism

The substantial growth of tourism activity clearly marks tourism as one of the most remarkable economic and social phenomena of the past century. Every year a bigger portion of the world population takes part in tourism activity and tourism has developed as one of the most dynamic and fastest growing economic sector for the majority of world countries.

In fact, tourism business accounts for 11% of the world's GDP. The number of international arrivals shows an evolution from a mere 25 million international arrivals in 1950 to the almost 715 million of 2002, corresponding to an average annual growth rate of 7 per cent. In the same period, international tourism receipts, at current prices and excluding international transport costs, had an average annual growth rate of 11 per cent.

Modern tourism is characterized by strong overall development and by a growing tendency for tourists to visit new destinations, together with tourism product diversification and increasing competition between destinations. New destinations are steadily increasing their market share.

By region, this growing dispersion of tourists is illustrated by above-average growth in the number of international tourist arrivals in East Asia and the Pacific, South Asia, Africa and the Middle East and by the below-average growth of the more traditional tourist-receiving regions of Europe and the Americas. Europe and the Americas are still the main tourist-receiving regions. From 1950 to 2000, international tourist arrivals in these two regions grew at an average annual growth rate of 6.6 and 5.9 per cent respectively.

In absolute terms, they registered an additional 387 million and 122 million arrivals with respect to the number registered in 1950. East Asia and the Pacific is the region which has most benefited from this transformation of the market. Historic series show that this region experienced the highest growth rate.

For many countries, both developed and developing, tourism is a very important source of foreign currency earnings and employment. Worldwide receipts amounted to US dollar 462 billion in 2001, which means $ 1.3 million or 1.4 billion a day. Compared to 2000 the receipts decreased -2.6 per cent from 474 billion. Expressed in euro international tourism receipts amounted to 516 billion, up 0.5 per cent from 514 billion in 2000. In 2001 US dollar appreciated 3 per cent compared to the euro (US$ 1.12 euro in 2001, 1.08 in 2000). Average receipts per arrival were $ 670 or . 750. About a half of all world's tourism receipts are earned in Europe.

In economic terms, international tourism receipts are classified as exports and international tourism expenditure as imports. In 1999, international tourism and international fare receipts accounted for roughly 8 per cent of total export earnings on goods and services worldwide. Total international tourism receipts, including those generated by international fares, amounted to an estimated US$ 555 billion, surpassing all other international trade categories.

Together with the earnings of foreign currency, tourism is also an important job supplier. Unfortunately, 6.6 million jobs worldwide have been lost in the tourism sector the last two years. The employment in tourism was rising at an annual growth rate of 4% during a couple of years, but from the year 2001 this slightly changed, according to figures of the International Labour Organization (ILO).

Provisional the ILO has no signs this will improve. The level of the year 2000 will be reached again in 2005 at the earliest. The impact of the terrorist attacks in Djerba, Bali and Mombassa on international tourism are not clear yet. The post-September 11 syndrome has also not yet been overcome but the facts prove the thesis that the economic situation in the world is a more powerful threat to international tourism than the fear of terrorism. So, the biggest problem in the current situation of world tourism is worldwide uncertainty. However, one thing remains certain: the economic success of countries positively influences both inbound tourism as well as outbound tourism. China is a shining example of this fact.

Tourism is one of the major European economical, cultural and social enterprises. However, information and support services for tourists are often inadequate. Usually, tourists have to move around in an unknown environment. Information about sites of tourist interest is often not easily available. The same holds for real-time information services, which take into account the changes in the environment (e.g. traffic).

The meaning of these services is to assist the tourist to move around the city and to identify service points. In the standard situations, tourists are in need of information in order to:

— Plan a visit (e.g. transportation, hotels, restaurants, sites of interest etc.);

— Navigate in the environment (e.g. trips in the city, traffic situation, parking availability etc.);

— Enjoy the sites they are visiting (e.g. historical and cultural information etc.);

— Find services in the environment (e.g. banks, pharmacies, public services etc.);

— Acquire detailed documentation about the visited sites after the visit.

Management of Cultual Changes

Travel and tourism are considered the most popular form of individual enjoyment in the countries of origin of the visitors. Despite this fact, the consequences of the steady growing tourism are often criticised by the citizens of these same countries. The ephemeral nature of the tourism phenomenon is a cause of insecurity; moreover, it is often subject to misleading, emotional and even ideologically-inspired interpretations.

As for the impact of tourism on local cultures and populations, this remains a highly controversial subject. For a better understanding of tourism we need first to clarify a few basic concepts and processes. To begin with, it would help to know just why "homo turisticus", the most important actor in the tourism process, needs to travel in the first place.

Furthermore, the consequences of the collision between different cultures needs to be assessed from the point of view of cultural and social sustainability. Finally we need to ask ourselves whether or not local cultural interactions would really respond to focused efforts to manage them. First however we need to understand how a tourism enterprise functions from a management point of view. And, most important of all, we need to clarify the role that regional and local authorities could play as representatives of the interests of resident populations.

Tourism and culture are two distinct phenomena that influence each other and that are both open to interpretation. The vagueness of the two concepts leaves room for original and often contradictory thinking. This can result in conflicting interpretations, often rooted in an ideological view of the dynamic and tense relationship between tourism and culture.

Tourism is an aspect of modern culture that in its most common form is understood as a system of relations that arise when individuals travel and stop over at various destinations to get away from the routine of normal daily life. The concept of tourism is more objective and empirically ascertainable than certain other cultural concepts.

The social, economic and spatial meaning of tourism can be described in terms of both ideas and physical realities. As a general term culture does not call to mind any immediately identifiable specific thing. Physical historic buildings that represent a large part of man's heritage are however very much a part of the concept of culture. The concept also includes a large number of symbols and rituals.

These are the more or less visible manifestations of ideological systems and views of the nature of the human being that are perceptible only to the intellect. They are based on inherited values, of which individuals and whole societies are often not consciously aware, and which are themselves the result of idealistic consensus.

The relationship between tourism and culture is extremely tense, both in theory and practice. Modern tourism has been the target of cultural criticism right from the start. Large numbers of tourists are as unwelcome as hordes of migrants, since they upset the normal cultural equilibrium of a society or a territorial entity.

Coming "from outside" society and having a high degree of visibility, they are not readily accepted. The greater their number the more disturbance they cause. The limits to the tolerance of visitors fall in the host areas in accordance with recognised group sociology mechanisms ("in-group/ out-group" mechanism). Critics see this apparent "mass phenomenon", which is basically a question of quantity or large numbers, as a threat to the intrinsic values of the host cultures.

The intrinsic value of cultural manifestations cannot be disputed. Unique cultural landscapes and cultural monuments are part of the history of all human being. They should not be sacrificed to tourists' appetite for new experiences. We cannot allow them to be trampled and destroyed by hordes of visitors. Indeed one of the fundamental duties of scientists and authorities is to alert the public to the potential negative cultural consequences of tourism.

It is also important that local resident populations make an effort to combat the negative externalities of tourism, which they are the first to perceive as excessive, since this is the only way in which they can protect their cultural identity. However, we need to bear in mind that tourism in all its permutations is a part of culture and must be accepted as such.

The meeting between a visitor and his or her host is one of the oldest forms of culture, which is governed by the necessary mechanisms for dealing with strangers in the least conflictual way possible. Travel and tourism also help to make individuals and society at large more aware of the need to protect and preserve existing cultural attractions.

Tourism's fundamental association with culture reflects the basic motivations of the people we call tourists. No economic theory can provide a satisfactory explanation, nor can such notions as the increased income and travel budget available to households, the comparative advantages of places, the competence of service providers, or the growth of networks in the field of product development and promotion, provide the answers.

The reasons people travel and the choice of destination are in fact meta-economic in most cases. People travel for immaterial cultural reasons that are beyond the logic of supply and demand. Travel motivation based on existing cultural differences remain of crucial importance for tourism. Most people travel to discover or rediscover something different, new and unique. In economic terms such differences create competitive advantages. They result in imperfect competition between destinations, since local cultures and cultural monuments are unique.

The reason a given destination is no longer in demand and no longer considered "fashionable" can often be found in the cultural roots of tourism. In most cases cultural resources are the foundations on which innovative tourism products and services are developed. Sustainable commercial success often depends on the availability of cultural resources able to create that all-important difference.

Very different cultures come together in a given tourism region. The four-cultures model shows how cultural exchanges work. The region of origin of the visitor determines his or her cultural self-awareness. It also determines the behaviour of individual tourists to a great extent. Generally speaking, visitors from the industrialised countries have a similar behavioural pattern.

Their objective is to get as far away as possible from the world of work and to find compensation in the leisure world of tourism for the things that are lacking in everyday life. But even when such visitors go on holiday the culture of their region of origin goes with them as a kind of ballast. The popularisation of tourism has however resulted in the development of a genuine tourism lifestyle, which includes all activities essential to preparing for and making the journey.

This has given rise to a kind of holiday culture, which is basically determined by the leisure society of the country of origin. Local residents at the travel destination, as "a minority who provides services", develop over a period of time a service culture, in which their own lifestyle is modified in accordance with the visitors' needs and interests. This culture reduces cultural confrontation since residents are used to dealing with visitors, particularly those directly involved in tourism.

Finally the cultural exchanges are also influenced by the original and traditional culture of the region and of the specific location. It is this that attracts visitors and also provides the basis for the identity of local residents.

Impact of globalisation

The irreversible process of globalisation has an ever greater impact on the relationship between tourism and culture at the local level, shrinking the world and promoting the emergence of a "global village" through intercontinental tourism, as the locomotive of a worldwide process of integration. Tourism of course does little more than to reinforce the other driving forces of globalisation at work in the world.

Thus, for example, the influence of the mass media on the emerging new world culture is considerably greater than that of tourism, since the latter is limited to certain times of the year and to specific areas. In any case, tourism and the new world culture are by now inseparable. The development of cultural similarities favoured by tourism introduces a note of banality and to some extent threatens existing resources based on cultural differences.

One common observable reaction to this conundrum is a renaissance of support for local cultural uniqueness and increasing concern about protecting traditional culture. With the growing internationalisation of everyday relations societies are beginning to recognise the importance of the roots that provide meaning and promote cohesion. Thus the more uniform the world seems to become, the stronger the resistance of those who try to defend and preserve local identity.

The levelling of world culture is thus counteracted by the rediscovery of local cultural differences. This local trend acts as a counter-force to the process of global integration. Suppliers of tourism products and services are having to make the best of the new situation. They are taking advantage of the similarities in the area of tourism preferences and supply-side standards of comfort and quality emerging around the world for an increasingly industrial production and marketing supported by information technology.

Globalisation is increasingly leading to design-oriented tourism products, which often combine traditional cultural goods and the achievements of modern civilisation. As the world becomes smaller a new view of cultural interaction in tourism regions becomes increasingly essential. The customary complaints of the civilisation critics need to be reconsidered.

A solution must be found to the old conflict between economic requirements and cultural concerns. Local cultures and identities must become more open, and must learn to adapt. What is needed above all is a better general understanding of the phenomenon of tourism.

Modern tourism is a very special sector of the economy. It is part of the emerging fourth sector, the so-called experience economy, which thanks to increases in productivity and prosperity made possible by information technology is providing an ever greater number of goods and services to meet immaterial needs in the areas of individual well-being and self-realisation.

These include, in particular, all cultural experiences. The experience economy thus creates additional employment and income. Tourism manufactures and markets very special experiences, which invariably have a cultural component. Tourism is like a dream factory, which oversimplifies reality. The potential visitors are attracted by inspiring dreams that are no more than stereotypes of reality.

These are the raw materials which economic actors use for the development and marketing of the final tourism products. Products are designed and brands created in order to stimulate these dreams and generate demand. Suppliers of tourism products and services popularise cultural content by appealing to the emotions. They make culture popular in ways that are far from ideal, from the strictly educational point of view.

They create a stereotyped dream destination on the basis of existing cultural resources. In this way they reduce the complexity of genuine traditional culture and create something that is closer to the stereotypes cherished by visitors. This involves the development of a new language of symbols, and ultimately results in the invention of a new tourism culture.

The "immaterial" of culture is integrated in the "materiel" of packaged tourism services. This package of services can then be marketed as a complete experience. The aim of the supplier of tourism products and services is to encourage the visitor to consume as much as possible through promotion based on images and the stage-managing of experiences.

From the economic point of view tourism is above all a business whose stock in trade is cultural differences and increasingly also cultural events, buildings and installations. From the point of view of human and cultural sciences this materialisation and commercialisation is regrettable. Existing cultural resources only become relevant from the point of view of tourism when put to economic use. This means turning them into attractions.

Attractions serve as the basis for the development and marketing of packages of tourism services. Their materialisation into tourism products renders them consumable. For those to whom culture is an end in itself this materialisation and commercialisation of cultural resources is a bitter pill to swallow. People often lose sight of the fact that a great many human activities are possible only because of the consumer at the end of the line.

In the widest sense consumption is a cultural act which provides meaning and can contribute to individual self-realisation. Critics should also need to be made aware of the fact that without the support of the economy the care and preservation of culture, and its further development, would scarcely be possible. From the economic point of view cultural resources are to be counted among the advantages of a location, which help to position a tourism destination in the market.

The problem of tourism and culture is refers to the effort required to protect humankind's traditional cultural heritage in its most genuine timeless and unique form, avoiding at the same time the creation of standardised cultural "pap". As the experience orientation of tourism becomes generalised, and increasingly encroaches on the cultural domain, this need is taking on a new dimension.

Indeed the conscious reception of cultural resources is invariably experience-oriented; they cannot be deep-frozen for consumption at some future date. Such experiences are almost always emotional, frequently served with more than a pinch of nostalgia and seen in the light of contemporary wisdom. In this age of globalisation the debate that has been going on since the 1970s about the cultural externalities of streams of visitors in less developed areas, needs to be rekindled.

To date, the culture shock which the open and largely unstructured lifestyle of visitors causes in the more or less closed local societies of the typical destination has been subject to criticism. Too little attention is paid to the fact that the demonstrative behaviour of these visitors not only causes shocks and confrontations but also provides experiences that are important for survival in our increasingly multicultural world.

In this sense, the tourism destination can be seen as a kind of intercultural laboratory for both visitors and local residents. In the more developed tourism regions increasing prosperity has brought greater understanding of the need to maintain local specificity and prevent the overexploitation of resources, as well as the resolve to do so. The traditional theory of acculturation, based on the assumption that the dominant culture will win in the end, can thus no longer be accepted at face value.

The impact of the touristic lifestyle on the workaday world of the local resident population, characterised by the demands of the workplace and the fight for survival, is not entirely effective. Moreover, the influence of tourism on the general development process is only one among others. It is also clear that globalisation, and the new world culture which it is creating, softens the impact of the local cultural confrontation.

Growing world integration is also having an impact on the local production and marketing of tourism services. Various studies have shown that customer expectations with regard to comfort and service quality are more or less the same all over the world. Of course, at the same time, visitors from different cultures continue to sleep, eat and drink in their own peculiar ways.

The levelling of customer expectations is above all a matter of the general "convenience" that an increasingly universal industrial service culture is able to guarantee. Nevertheless, potential visitors to traditional tourism regions expect typical local elements of differentiation to be included in the tourism products on offer. The supplier thus creates an additional benefit that is increasingly noticed and appreciated by the visitor.

Needless to say it is by no means easy for the small-to-medium tourism enterprises (SMEs) of traditional destinations to successfully meet international standards of comfort while at the same time respecting differences in cultural practices and integrating local characteristics in their products. The inclusion of local elements in the tourist service culture in any case requires participation of the local population in the production process.

The negative experiences of tourism centres created "ex nihilo" show that this is the only way to ensure a typical local atmosphere. The ruins of ancient monuments are a reminder of the transient nature of man and of his cultural creations. Despite occasional ideologically inspired atrocities such as the wanton destruction of the Buddha statues in Afghanistan, cultural resources, and buildings in particular, are generally distinguished by their longevity.

They outlive both political systems and economic cycles. Cultural monuments are the most timeless tourist attractions of all. Even so, given the great number of such attractions, there is a fundamental problem of care and maintenance, which has to do with the general development of civilisations and not just with tourism. In Italy, for example, a land rich in cultural history, there are so many thousands of churches, palaces and other historic buildings, both privately and publicly owned, that it is impossible even for such a prosperous economy to maintain them properly, and many are therefore doomed to crumble into ruins.

Less sustainable is the utilisation of cultural attractions when they are visited by too many tourists or excursionists. Well-known attractions are indeed often inundated by visitors. The world's main culture capitals, as well as the attractions in developing countries and emerging economies, all have the same problem controlling the "throughput" of visitors. In many cases visitors come and go without the benefit of an enjoyable culture experience, disappointed in the quality of the offer.

It is not possible to manage the cultural exchange between visitors and the resident population in the same way as one manages a company or an organization, nor would it be worth attempting. It is more a question of monitoring this open, dynamic and complex process, and setting the necessary framework conditions. This will require for all stakeholders a new understanding of culture and tourism as well as clear ideas about the role to be played by each individual actor who participates in the cultural interactions.

Multicultural identity

Ensuring the greatest possible cultural diversity is not only necessary for the well-being of the human race, it is also a prerequisite for economic success in tourism. Meeting the objective in this age of globalisation requires taking a fresh look at the traditional concept of cultural identity. A society that is wrapped up in its own values, and that takes too negative a view of differences and looks unfavourably on all things foreign is out of step with today's world. It is no longer an option to live in "splendid isolation". Too much concern about one's own identity is harmful, leading to ethnocentricity and making it impossible to "live and let live".

Paradoxically, visitors are the first to seek the greatest possible cultural differences and to want to preserve picturesque "cultural backwardness". Their ideal is a real-life museum. The age of dialogue between cultures has already begun in the tourism regions. Basically it seems that in this increasingly networking world we are no longer able to distinguish between the things that originate in local cultures and the things such cultures absorb from the outside.

The same people who have reservations when it comes to foreign visitors and the way they behave may have already unconsciously adopted foreign cultural practices themselves. They may eat like Italians, love American jazz or classical music from Vienna, and dress like Parisians. Cultural identity only makes sense today if it is open to the world and gravitates towards an identity that incorporates many multicultural facets.

Today's "civilised human being" must be ready to accept foreignness as an opportunity and must be ready to take the best from the great variety of cultural possibilities. It is also time for a new understanding of tourism, which from the holistic point of view of the visitor is a complete experience. The job of the supplier of tourism products and services is to reconcile the motivations of potential visitors with the available local resources.

A more demanding task however is to manage the entire chain of tourism services including transport, overnight accommodation, catering, entertainment and cultural activities - as a single package. Tourism management is today a fine-tuned business process. Design, image-building and promotion are tailor-made to ensure that the needs of all potential visitors are met.

The package of tourism services is planned, developed and above all stage-managed in situ just like a play or a film. The crux of the matter to make the travel and the stay as attractive as possible for the visitor. Among other things this requires a "front stage", a hearty welcome and customised services. Meanwhile "back stage" it is necessary to ensure that everything runs just as smoothly for the customer, and with the help of cost-effective technology will be as productive as possible.

Tourism requires management skills combining "high touch" with "high tech". Those who manage cultural interaction need the support of a new understanding of culture and tourism. They must know how to address the needs and interests of a variety of "stakeholders". These include not just visitors but also the resident population, the local authorities and various tourism industry representatives.

As for the visitor, the principle that applies in tourism as a buyer's market remains that of "the customer is king". But the visitor must nonetheless be careful to respect the local environment, an ability which in most cases depends on family background ("upbringing") and experience as a traveller. A minimum of tourism ethics is also needed to ensure that visitors behave in a responsible manner.

Successful contacts with the local population also serve as a cultural learning process and create meaning for the individual tourist. Tourism experiences can also have an impact on everyday life including on a visitor's professional skills and abilities, and can thus bring advantages to an increasingly internationalised economy. It is beyond a doubt that successful tourism development also benefits the local resident population both socially and economically.

Tourism creates jobs and income. It improves awareness of local traditions and of natural as well as cultural resources. However, local populations also have to put up with certain disadvantages of tourism development. For tourism can cause local rents to rise, and create traffic and transport problems. One also needs to be prepared for an acceleration of the processes of change at the social and cultural levels.

Handling these problems successfully requires a significant increase in local tourism awareness. Efforts to familiarise the local population with the "ins and outs" of tourism need to begin at school with children. They must learn that attitudes of openness and friendliness in dealing with visitors contribute enormously to the quality of local tourism products and services.

The political authorities and the media, as representatives of the general public, play a leading part in the management of cultural interactions. It is on their ability to understand tourism that the preservation of existing cultural resources and the ability to make the best use of a location's multicultural openness will depend. Only a well-informed media and political establishment can ensure the necessary protection of cultural resources and the reduction of prejudices against visitors.

Finally, the role of the tourism industry in the area of cultural interaction should not be underestimated. The readiness to cooperate and to innovate in a given tourism location depends on the "spirit of enterprise" of all local economic actors. This is important, since the development and marketing of tourism products and services is possible only through a successful partnership involving the various suppliers.

Above all there is a need for the greatest possible autonomy at the level of the local authority, as the most important platform for the implementation of tourism policy. The local authority must be in a position, in accordance with the principle of subsidiarity, to closely monitor the tourism development process.

The higher authorities should do their utmost to ensure that local authorities are given the necessary planning authority and revenue sources. It is equally important to ensure the full democratic participation of the entire local resident population in the most important decisions concerning new tourism projects.

Tourism entrepreneurs are key partners for the local authorities. Experience has shown that vertical cooperation involving all tourism service providers working through a local tourism organization is likewise essential. This is the platform on which the destination management approach is developed and perfected.

This approach is based on the assumption that a tourism location can be managed in the same way as a cruise ship. More recent studies have shown however that there are limits to vertical integration, and that it is no longer possible to manage the bigger resorts like Cancun as a single enterprise. It has also been shown that the success of integrated resorts depends to some extent on their ability to take into consideration the concerns of the constituent communities.

Local tourism organizations are particularly well suited to the task of creating an effective "public/private partnership" between local authorities and the private sector. They have the advantage of being close to both the citizenry and the market. Such organizations make it possible for the majority of local service providers, which are small-to-medium enterprises, to approach the market with the extra strength of a partnership.

These organizations can provide effective protection against the market power of the international tourism industry actors including the big tour operators and hotel chains, which with their transnational strategies are able to take full advantage of local development potential.

Influence of Culture on Economic Policy

There are deeply rooted values that differ between cultures and have a significant impact on the way societies are organized, what role government plays, and how the various organizations within societies work. These differences are often seriously underestimated. As a result, international organizations, universities and governments often assume that approaches that have been successfully applied elsewhere will be successful everywhere. In practice, this is extremely doubtful, to say the least.

Experience has shown that if change processes are undertaken in a way that goes against deeply rooted beliefs and values, people and organizations can perhaps be forced to act in a certain way for a short period of time. However, as soon as the situation has been normalized, the natural inclination will be to revert to "old" approaches.

An understanding of the fundamental cultural values would explain why apparently unrelated issues can be traced back to the same basic principles. It can also help to explain systematic differences in political systems, economic systems and management practices, for example between the United States, Japan, France, Mexico and the Netherlands. Many problems arise when debates on important social policy issues such as the economy, proceed from an implicit assumption that culture is secondary to rational technical argument.

Underestimating the significance of culture and its consequences on policy can lead to some unusual conclusions. For instance, the report "Institutions, values, standards and growth" by the Nijenrode Forum for

Economic Research (NYFER) of the Economics department of Nijenrode University in the Netherlands. "With the whole world writing admiringly about the Dutch economic miracle," NYFER's report warns, "of the six original EU states, the Netherlands is the shabbiest". He adds:

"Belgium's constitutional state is considerably less stable than that of the Netherlands and its politics are being poisoned by stalemates between the Flemish and the Walloons, yet statistics show Belgium to be richer than the Netherlands". The interesting point is that both of NYFER's statements contain a grain of truth. In comparison with many surrounding countries, the Netherlands has succeeded in keeping labor costs low, achieving a flexible job market and modernizing the social security system.

For instance, there is a discrepancy between NYFER's claim that the United Kingdom has a higher average level of wealth than the Netherlands and The Economist's observation that: "The EU members poorer than the Union average were the Finns, Britons, Irish, Spaniards, Portuguese and Greeks". NYFER's report states that their study was based on the proposition in an increasing number of studies that culture does have an effect on economic growth. They refer to two recent published works claiming that "countries have a stronger competitive position in the world economy if their citizens have more trust in one another".

This proposition is subsequently linked to the "dataset" of World Values Survey, which contains descriptions of value orientations of the citizens of a large number of countries. More detailed analysis in the study is limited to a comparison of approximately 20 prosperous OECD countries with respect to seven indicators: lack of public morality, law-abidance, permissiveness, post-materialism, intolerance, trust in institutions, and trust in humanity.

Culture has not always been popular as a source of explanations for behavior. Of course, culture cannot be used as an explanation for everything that takes place in society. Life is far too complex to pretend that one-dimensional explanations can adequately map the human condition. Human behavior is not always predictable. However, as people become aware of themselves in relation to their environment, they are able to make new choices.

In psychology, these are called mind-sets. Mind-sets are values that both give direction to new behavior and set its boundaries. We can also find cultural mind-sets in history. Culture is defined as the collective, mental programming which distinguishes one group or category of people from another. This programming, or mind-set, influences patterns of thought, which are reflected in the meaning people give to the different aspects of their lives, and therefore help shape the institutions of a society.

This does not mean that everyone in a particular society is "programmed" in exactly the same way. There are considerable individual differences. But when fundamental values of various societies are compared, "majority preferences" are found to exist, and to recur again and again as a result of the way children are brought up by their parents and the educational system. When we examine how societies organize themselves, these majority preferences turn out to have a modifying influence at both the micro and macro levels.

They appear to have an influence on the ways in which good leadership is defined, on how the decision-making process is structured, and on the way people monitor how policies are implemented; in short, everything that has to do with organizational behavior. The problem is that a great many people do not recognize these "gross group" descriptions as having an influence and being consistent over time.

On average, individuals tend to feel that they are very different from their parents, and their grandparents are very different from their own parents. The reason for this "true" observation is that it is usually the visible aspects of culture that are compared. In so doing, it appears to be easy to establish that the clearly visible behavior of the present generation is different from the behavior of past generations.

The mind-set approach can be used to gain insight into what is different and what is consistent. Our parents and grandparents behaved differently because they lived in totally different conditions. The world is changing rapidly and we are being forced to adjust to these changes and to develop new behavior. But the development of this new behavior is constantly influenced by the set of collective preferences that we have designated as mind-sets.

This concept may appear to be "as soft as butter". It is true that there is some hesitation at the international level, and even resistance, to employing these cultural explanations; some people even see them as a cloak for obscure deterministic arguments. Cultures that score low on power distance create, from the moment children can talk, an environment that whereby parents give signals such as "tell us what you think; express yourself; you have a brain, so speak your mind".

By doing this, parents, the fist power holder in the life of children, are trying to communicate that children are entitled to speak their mind, even in the presence of power holders. Thus, the real underlying message is: "you are independent and autonomous in your relation to power holders". Teachers in such cultures have the same attitude. They invite the students to enter into discussion, both with each other and with their teachers. It is even appreciated and rewarded if a student, with good arguments of course, tries to refute what a teacher claims.

Cultures that score high on power distance create an environment in which the first signal from the parents to a child is: "you must primarily respect the older generation. If you would like to say something, you can politely raise your hand and if you are granted permission, you may politely ask a question or make a comment". The central message is: "you are dependent on power holders".

Teachers have the same role in these cultures. Normally they stand in front of the class and impart their knowledge to the group. Now and then pupils are given the opportunity to politely ask questions. This results in an entirely different atmosphere. The educational objectives are also entirely different, e.g. reproduction of knowledge and not the development of an open or critical mind.

These two systems have a fundamental effect on the conduct of people in organizations. One of the consequences is the way in which people act in meetings. The expectations of what a meeting should be are, in fact, quite different. People from cultures with a lower power distance (e.g. the Dutch, Americans, English, Swedes, Danes, Norwegians, Germans) expect meetings to be places where people can have open discussions, defend their interests and eventually decide on actions, strategies or policy together.

The general view is that people who do not speak up at a meeting lose their right to be obstructive afterwards. Therefore, the level of irritation with respect to people who do not subsequently comply with what has been agreed during the meeting is extremely high. In countries that score high on power distance (France, Belgium, Portugal, Greece, Russia and practically all developing countries), meetings are expected to be places where power holders are given the opportunity to inform others about their plans, ideas or strategies and the others are allowed to politely ask questions.

The leadership styles in these two types of culture are totally different. In countries that score low on power distance, managers tend to be invisible. If they are is too visible and constantly look over people's shoulders, that will demotivate people. In countries that score high on power distance, managers are expected to motivate their employees. When decisions have been made, they explain how they want them implemented by means of clear task descriptions and instructions.

They subsequently verify whether everything has been done according to plan. In short, an attitude which irritates both parties in countries that score low on power distance. However, this attitude should not be misunderstood for authoritarian behavior, which is detested all over the world; it could be called instead, paternalistic behavior: top-down, but with awareness for the needs of people.

There is a greater than average need for independence in these cultures. Hierarchy is interpreted as an "inequality" of roles in society and in institutions, which is used for the convenience of communication and decision-making. But in principle power holders have the same feeling about subordinates as subordinates have about power holders: "they are people like you and me".

As a result, people in these cultures feel less threatened and are more willing to trust others; there is more underlying harmony between people with power and those without. Hence, the adage "no news is good news" applies to the communication between the various echelons in society and in organizations.

In these cultures, people have, on average, a greater need for dependence. Hierarchy is interpreted more as an "existential inequality": there must be an order of "inequality" in which everyone finds his or her rightful place. "Bosses" (superiors, managers) consider subordinates to be another kind of people and want to be treated respectfully by them.

Subordinates also consider superiors to be another kind and regard them with potential distrust. The consequences of these attitudes are that there is always a dormant conflict between people with power and those without, due to a lack of basic trust; "no news is good news" is less so due to the underlying distrust.

Therefore the power holders are more inclined to check the implementation of rules and laws. Mental images are fundamental social structures that we all have in our minds. They transcend all types of activity and delve deeper than differences in an organization culture. Both in the private and public sector, among those employed in the uniformed services and in welfare departments, people from the same culture have a similar image of the way society works.

The consequence of this is that if two different mental images are operational between two cultures where one communal language is spoken, as is the case with the Netherlands and Flanders, this can lead to major problems. The different images lead to misunderstandings and differences in appreciation with regard to desired styles of leadership, desired degree of centralization, reward systems, etc. The six mental images are: the contest model, the network, the pyramid, the Solar system, the family, and the well-oiled machine.

This image is applicable to the Anglo-Saxon countries. The cultural context of this mental image is: low power distance, lower uncertainty avoidance and high individuality. The central assumption of this mental image is: if you give people and organizations the freedom to compete with each other, something good will always come out of it.

The characteristic of this organization outline is that hierarchy is not seen as an existential difference between people, but as something that is agreed among people to facilitate the work in organizations; it should be clear who is delegating to whom and who is reporting to whom.

In principle, employers and subordinates negotiate about objectives, targets and work content. Targets are very important because people experience them as a challenge. No one should "fiddle" with targets once they have been formulated, since they function as the central element of performance monitoring.

The assessment of the targets set beforehand is the foundation for work motivation. People are rewarded for their performance as measured against the targets fixed. The reward is given in the form of bonuses or career moves. Solutions to problems are achieved by communicating with each other. Open competition is central in this model. In order to motivate people, they must be able to compete with others, but also with themselves. In this model, important concepts include achievement, target setting, winners and losers, making it, career, bonus systems, and special career paths for "high potentials".

There is a trap in the tendency to give these theories and concepts a universal value. The management theories that are taught at universities and business schools around the world mainly stem from Anglo Saxon scholars. The explanation for this is a commonly human one. The inclination exists to imitate the conduct of economically successful people. This is true all over the world with respect to US culture. People drink Coca-Cola, and there is even a McDonalds on the Square of Heavenly Peace in Peking.

These people constitute, as it were, a symbol for progress and success. US management ideas are blindly adopted by managers everywhere. Some well-known consequences of this situation for organizations are the introduction, inter alia, of flexible reward systems, career-oriented management development systems, "management by objectives", and special training courses for "high potentials". Other consequences are that people partly adjust to the new "rituals".

In United kingdom, two strong political parties can be seen as a logical consequence of the first "mind-set". These compete with each other in a strongly polarized manner and accept that after the elections the "winner takes all", i.e. control of the entire government, including the top officials. In the Netherlands and Sweden, governments are already formed and there is no change in top officials.

Such fundamental differences in approach between these to systems can also be seen in other areas: insights into the role of the government, the approach to unemployment, the role of social security, and the role of trade unions are almost diametrically opposed. In order to illustrate the significance of these differences, it is worth examining the attitudes of two very different approaches to solving some of the problems governments experience all over the world.

All economies produce most goods and services for domestic consumption. So, even if an economy is not at all competitive, it is still "business as usual". If two companies are competing with each other, one wins and the other loses. If two economies are competing with each other, both can win, thanks to the law of comparative advantage.

While an organization which is not very competitive is not able to lower costs, an economy that is not very competitive is able to do so, for example by depreciating the currency after a period of high inflation. Krugman's conclusion is that an important criterion for an economy to be competitive is domestic productivity, in other words, output per worker. If this is taken as the standard, more factors come into play than only the drive to succeed alone.

The level of education in a country, the degree of innovation, political stability, and, for example, the number of strike days are found to be important. In these circumstances, network countries do not appear to be doing so badly. The degree of "femininity" of a society in a cultural sense relates, among other things, to an unwillingness to think in terms of winners and losers.

An important characteristic of "feminine" societies is that there is a great deal of sympathy for and solidarity with the underdog, irrespective of whether they are part of the family or ethnic group. This can be demonstrated from the official statistics regarding foreign aid as a percentage of the GDP.

In these countries, social and political conflicts lead to developments that inhibit growth. A study by US economist, discusses which elements affect growth. The study gives three reasons:

(a) Greater inequality in income leads to less education;

(b) Unequal division of income leads to an increase in the number of poor people. They do not have money - and cannot borrow it - to give their children a good education. This is particularly true of secondary education. Further-more, less inequality in income will lead to a reduction in the number of births, because people will be inclined to invest more in the education of fewer children, instead of having more children;

(c) Greater inequalities in income can also lead to political instability. Large differences between poor and rich can lead to crime, revolts etc. This political instability leads to an unwillingness by individuals to invest, and that is bad for the economy.

The cultural context in relation to income inequality and poverty deserves further analysis. Discussion on income inequality is also taking place in the US, but this has little to do with a change in values. According to a survey published in American Enterprise Magazine in 1990, less than a third of Americans questioned said that they thought the Government should do something about income inequality. As may be expected of a country with a market mind-set, even the "have-nots" support the idea of inequality. The idea apparently is: "I have nothing now, but I may win the lottery next week. And if I do, I in principle against having to hand over this money".

The problem of many in the US is not so much that income inequality is growing. The unease is caused by the fact that poor people have become much poorer in absolute terms in the last 20 years. By way of illustration, the poorest people are 11 per cent worse off in income terms, while the richest 10 per cent of the population are 18 per cent better off.

But a political majority can never be found to stop the solidarity with the financially weaker people in these countries. People talk about discouraging misuse of resources and the problem of long-term affordability. But there is always support. The motives in countries that score high on uncertainty avoidance are entirely different. And high uncertainty avoidance is what countries such as France, Belgium, Germany and Switzerland have in common.

The support for social programmes in these countries has little to do with sympathy for those worse off; it is rather the result of a focus on social order. If the differences between the poor and the rich are too great, society becomes unpredictable. The prevailing consensus thus is not so much influenced by solidarity as by fear of losing social cohesion, which will lead to social disorder.

The network model is seen in action with its emphasis on consensus, support and common interests.

A complaint heard from market economists is that the network model is ineffective in combating unemployment. However, poverty does not always rise if unemployment rises. Poverty figures in the rich industrialized countries have remained stable practically everywhere, while unemployment fluctuated.

Cantillon concludes that poverty is directly influenced by social security. Countries that are willing to invest in social security generally have low levels of poverty. The effect of different mental images can also be seen here: countries that uphold the competition model have a low unemployment rate, but high levels of poverty.

Cantillon demonstrates that poverty in all OECD countries will increase if social security is further reduced. The conclusion is that an increasing proportion of the population in the OECD countries is unable to rise above the poverty line through work alone. The danger of this development is that it leads to the formation of an underclass. In Europe, the majority of the unemployed are white. But the effect in both cases is long-term unemployment with as a resulting polarization and marginalization.

However, even if unemployment in Europe is not fundamentally a race issue, first and second generation immigrants have often had a particularly hard time. Twenty to thirty years ago, they came to the West European countries to do the work nobody else wanted to do. Many of these jobs have since disappeared, and they and their children are now finding it very hard to adjust. Unemployment sometimes takes the form of spatial separation. People on the wrong side of the line start to cut themselves off from society.

For example, in the Netherlands a disproportionate number of the long-term unemployed have ex-directory phone numbers. This voluntary segregation is dangerous, because it represents a loss of the feeling of mutual involvement and mutual responsibility. The problem in Europe as well as in the US is that if the middle classes disappear from an inner city and only the poor are left behind, this leads to a downward spiral of urban decline.

The only people who want to live there are those who cannot go anywhere else. Burglaries and violence increase as frustrated youths turn to drugs and crime. And, as unemployed men are less marriageable, the number of extramarital children rises and the growth in the numbers of one-parent families creates a new hard core of dependence. The fact that this can threaten public order was made clear in the spate of inner-city riots and looting across the US in the "long hot summers" of the late 1960s, as well as in Los Angeles in the early 1990s.

Furthermore, the middle classes are retreating to their fortified suburbs. The overlap of concentrations of urban decline and immigrant communities also creates an easy target for political extremists. Before proceeding to an analysis of these circumstances, it should be stated, regarding the discussion on work and employment, that it is very important to maintain a distinction between the economic and cultural aspects of the discussion about unemployment, inequality and poverty.

The Netherlands is one of the most "feminine-oriented" countries in the world. One of the consequences of this is a different attitude toward work. People are very interested in the quality of life. In employment terms this means that people do not "live to work" but rather "work to live". Indeed, one of the reasons why the

Dutch work force is relatively flexible is because many people work part-time.

Many economists have maintained that, even in objective economic terms, democracy is the best system. Only democracy can ensure long-term economic freedom. Ownership rights for example, are safeguarded by independent leaders or regimes.

In Australia, promotion is a key area of government funding for tourism. It is argued that, without government funding, tourism promotion would be significantly less than optimal. Commonwealth, State and Territory agencies involved in tourism marketing often leverage public funds through cooperative arrangements with private sector operators.

The Australian Tourist Commission, which is jointly funded by the Commonwealth Government and industry, is Australia's primary inbound tourism marketing agency. Its principle objectives under the Australian Tourist Commission Act 1987 are to:

— increase the number of visitors to Australia from overseas,

— maximise the benefits to Australia from overseas visitors, and

— in meeting these objectives, work with other relevant agencies to promote the principles of ecologically sustainable development and raise awareness of the social and cultural impacts of international tourism in Australia.

Working with the private sector and State and Territory tourism authorities, the Australian Tourist Commission's activities include television, print and electronic advertising, public relations and information programs, and the coordination of Australian industry participation in international trade events.

The Australian Tourist Commission also plays a role in product development and retail travel agent education programs as well as providing input into government and industry policies that affect tourism. While over the past four years the Australian Tourist Commission has received record levels of funding from the Commonwealth Government, there have been calls for even higher levels of funding for the agency.

Industry's direct contribution to the Australian Tourist Commission's funding has declined in recent years and currently represents less than one third of total funding. The industry's indirect contribution for 2001-02 amounted to around $42 million. Total industry contribution appears to have declined since the pre-Olympic Games year, 1999-2000.

A number of other public agencies, such as Austrade and Invest Australia, are involved in promoting Australia. The Commonwealth Department of Foreign Affairs and Trade is the lead agency promoting Australia, with 83 overseas posts regularly engaging in promotional activities. Austrade, an agency within the Department of Foreign Affairs and Trade portfolio is working with individual tourism operators to promote its services in overseas markets and has recently appointed an industry specialist with the responsibility for the tourism sector who works closely with the industry in key export forums.

The Department of Education, Science and Training coordinates international education activities with accompanying benefits for tourism. The activities of these agencies are aimed primarily at enhancing Australia's international image. Success in these areas can influence not only perceptions of Australia as a tourism destination, particularly for business travellers, but also the attractiveness of Australia's tourism industry to foreign investors.

The various State and Territory tourism organisations are also involved in marketing Australia's attractions overseas. Funding levels vary according to State and Territory priorities and the importance of tourism to their economies. In addition, tourism operators are involved in marketing Australia by promoting their own tourism products and services.

State and Territory agency funding is sourced from direct government appropriation and other sources, including industry. Over the period 1995-96 to 1999-2000 there has been an overall increase of 33 per cent in government funding for tourism promotion in the States and Territories. Over the same period other sources of funding have increased by 13 per cent.

With the exception of Queensland, government funding in each State and Territory exceeds funding from other sources. International visitors may be of the perception that they have 'seen' Australia once they have visited its cities and major icon destinations. Improved promotion of regional destinations, such as the Kimberley, the West Coast of Tasmania, Kakadu, the Flinders Ranges, Broken Hill, Tropical North Queensland and the south west of Western Australia, has the potential to increase the length of visitor stays for both domestic and international visitors and encourage repeat visits.

Greater cooperation and coordination between Commonwealth, State and Territory programs could ensure that there is neither duplication nor gaps in the provision of services. In seeking to develop international business-either through increasing the number of international visitors or in pursuing consultancy or service delivery opportunities in overseas markets-it is possible that Australian tourism businesses will encounter various market access issues.

For example, there may be overseas regulations or rules which limit foreign companies or individuals from setting up subsidiaries or branch offices in Australia. There may also be taxes or impediments on Australian promotional material or restrictions on advertising in individual markets. In addition there may be structural, information and communication, or industry distribution factors that might impede Australian tourism businesses from developing market share.

International air service landing rights have been identified as a major market access issue. At the multilateral level, Australian industry is being consulted on impediments that can be taken up within the World Trade Organisation General Agreement on Trade in Services negotiations over the next few years. Also at the regional level, the Government has worked closely with Asia-Pacific Economic Cooperation counterparts to develop action plans to remove impediments to the sustainable growth of tourism in its region.

There are other significant international tourism organisations, such as the World Tourism Organisation, which engage in understanding tourism developments globally and promoting positive policy outcomes. Australia is not currently a member of the World

Tourism Organisation although Australian representatives do participate in some its activities.

At the bilateral level, the Commonwealth Government has worked closely with Australian industry and the Chinese government and has become the first country outside East Asia to reach an Approved Destination Status arrangement, which enables Chinese tourists to more easily visit Australia. The Government is also currently working closely with industry in studying factors which may be restricting Australia's capacity to capture a larger share of the Japanese market.

Leisure tourism has a wide range of tourism products aimed at meeting the needs of a diverse and sophisticated world travelling public. Inbound tourism operators put together package deals for international tourists visiting Australia and have well established business relationships with international cruise operators and duty free shopping operators, which utilise the 'closed bag' duty and tax-free system in parallel with the Tourist Refund Scheme.

The cruise shipping sector is a growing high yield sector which, during the peak Olympic year, saw around 90 cruise vessels visit Australia, collectively carrying 60,000 international visitors. Marine tourism, including bare boats and other charter vessels, is a substantial industry right around Australia, highlighted by tourism in the Great Barrier Reef Marine Park, which is estimated to generate $844 million per annum.

Built tourism attractions include permanent outdoor attractions, such as major theme parks, amusement parks and animal or marine based parks, transportable attractions, such as shows, carnivals and circuses, and indoor attractions, such as arts, culture, leisure and entertainment centres.

Increasingly, tourists are attracted by Australia's diverse and rich natural environment, and ecotourism has emerged as a significant industry sector, founded on Australia being one of only 17 mega-diverse countries on Earth, with many plants, animals and microorganisms living in no other country. The figures can be large-the Great Barrier Reef supports around 2 000 fish species and 500 coral species. This uniqueness and diversity is the backbone for Australia's nature based and ecotourism products.

During the 1990s the ecotourism sector became highly specialised and it now offers tourists world class ecotourism experiences, incorporating a high standard of environmental and cultural interpretation. It works closely with park management agencies, some of which have community involvement in their management through boards and committees. Examples of joint management by Indigenous landowners and park services include the Kakadu Board of Management and Parks Australia, and the Uluru-Kata Tjuta Board of Management and Parks Australia.

There are opportunities for government agencies, such as Austrade, Invest Australia and the Australian Tourist Commission to become more active in promoting more target markets, such as business tourism.

Market segments and niches

The last decade has seen the emergence and growth of a number of specialised niche tourism markets, which are offering new opportunities for tourism operators around Australia.

Business tourism expenditure, which includes visitors who may have a holiday in conjunction with a business trip, was around $11.2 billion in 1999. Of this, international business tourism records an expenditure of around $893 million. The meetings, incentives, conferences and exhibitions sector is one of the tourism industry's highest yielding sectors, worth around $6 billion a year.

The growth of the meetings industry has been explosive in Australia-140 international meetings were held here in 2000. Sydney is in the top three cities internationally for meetings and events, having welcomed 44 000 participants in 1999, behind only Vienna's 46 000 and Berlin's 73 000.

While backpacking is a long established niche market, it grew particularly rapidly in size and significance during the last decade, to become a major market segment. The latest available figures indicate that in 1999-2000, around 423 000 international backpackers visited Australia, with an average length of stay of 69 nights, and spent a total of $1.9 billion.

Sports tourism is emerging as an important market segment, for both participants and spectators. Australia's premier sporting event of recent times, the Sydney 2000 Olympic Games, was estimated by the Tourism Forecasting Council to have yielded Australia an extra 1.6 million international visitors, generating an additional $6.1 billion in tourism earnings. It should be noted that the bulk of these additional visitors were the result of Olympic Games publicity rather than direct tourism promotion.

Recent years have also seen the advent of the Masters Games and an increasing trend towards 'manufactured events', with tourism operators and sporting organisations working together to maximise the commercial benefits of sporting events. Examples include tourism packages for golfers and triathletes, and adventure tourism packages including whitewater rafting and bungee jumping.

The many and various sporting venues across Australia also provide facilities for other tourism events, such as concerts. Wine and food tourism has become popular in the many winegrowing regions of Australia, so much so that the Winemakers' Federation of Australia has identified wine tourism as a priority in its 30-year development strategy.

A national wine tourism strategy, supported by industry and governments, has been developed and is being implemented . A review of wine tourism and wine exports will soon be under way with a view to identifying specific opportunities and impediments. Further expansion of wine tourism offers the potential to create tourism hubs across many areas of regional Australia, for food and accommodation providers and other tourism related businesses.

'Farm stay' is also emerging as a growing market segment and is providing many of Australia's primary producers with opportunities to supplement farm income. Better alignment of this sector with other market segments would help strengthen its emerging growth potential. The importance of cultural tourism to tourism consumption is well documented.

For example, more than 40 per cent of international visitors to Australia purchased art and craft items, while spending on Aboriginal arts and craft products accounted for more than 50 per cent of all art and craft expenditure. In addition, in 1997, total international visitor expenditure on art and craft items was $296 million of which $155 million was on Aboriginal art and craft.

Australia's national cultural institutions are established attractions to both the national and international tourist markets. For example, over 2 million people (incorporating locals, interstate and overseas visitors) visited Canberra's cultural institutions in 2000-2001. Since its opening in March 2001, the National Museum of Australia has attracted almost 1 million people and the National Library of Australia's exhibition "Treasures of the Worlds Great Libraries" gained unprecedented popularity, attracting large numbers of visitors from interstate.

Research and statistics compiled by the Bureau of Tourism Research have revealed that one in two international visitors seek at least one cultural experience during their stay. The impact of this on related tourism industries (transport, hospitality, and retail) is substantial. Moreover, previous research has highlighted the importance of networks in obtaining and marketing information on cultural events and attractions and that a principal challenge is to stimulate interest in and possible future visits to cultural attractions.

Increasingly, tourists seeking nature based experiences are looking for Indigenous interpretations of the surrounding country and landscape, even in capital cities, where there is also significant potential for the development of Aboriginal Arts and Culture Centres. Growing interest in Indigenous tourism among international tourists has been reinforced in very recent times by the publication of a Lonely Planet guide to Aboriginal Australia.

The Tjapukai Indigenous theme park in Cairns is a world recognised interpretative facility. Indigenous arts and crafts constitute a major industry, with an estimated total market value of upwards of $173.4m in 1996-97. While the nature and degree of the impacts of tourism on Indigenous communities are not well understood by the mainstream tourism industry, it is increasingly becoming recognised that tourism, appropriately managed, can have positive economic, social and environmental benefits.

This recognition is reflected in the recent formation of a national leadership group, the Indigenous Tourism Leadership Group, composed of Indigenous and non-Indigenous business people and Commonwealth Government representatives, which is working to encourage the development of the Indigenous tourism sector and employment of Indigenous people in the wider tourism industry.

This Group was a private sector initiative arising from a National Indigenous Tourism Forum held in June 2000. There are also significant opportunities for tourism products aimed at particular groups in the community, for example, seniors tourism, tourism for people with disabilities, and tourism aimed at 'enthusiast' niche markets.

Other niche markets include educational tourism, arts and cultural tourism, defence and military tourism, health tourism and bare boats and other charter vessels. There are significant opportunities for tourism to play a greater role in education beyond traditional school excursions and to offer interpretation and broader education for children, including through vocational education and training.

These opportunities extend to adult education, particularly through the provision of arts and cultural experiences. Greater health consciousness in the wider community is opening up opportunities for health resorts and tourism products with a focus on healthy lifestyles. English language study tourism is an important niche market which has the potential to be a gateway to other areas of adult study tourism.

A recent survey conducted by English Australia for Australian Education International shows there is capacity to at least double language study tourism in 2003. Language study tourism has a significant regional presence, particularly in Queensland, and has considerable potential for development in other regions.

According to the 1999 Survey of International Students Finishing a Course of Study in Australia, 52 per cent of students finishing a course of study had relatives or friends visit them from their home country while in Australia. An average of 4.5 people visited each of those students during their period of study.

Despite perceptions by some institutions engaged in the education export industry that a strong emphasis on tourism may interfere with perceptions of Australia as a serious study destination, other institutions promote lifestyle as part of the package as do some regions. Indeed, there are flow-on benefits to Australia's education export sector from expanding recognition of Australia as an attractive tourist destination.

Collateral publicity from events, cultural exposure and educational or scientific exchange adds considerable value to Australia's international tourism marketing efforts and helps open up new opportunities for tourism growth from key markets. The more international successes that Australians can generate across a wide spectrum of endeavours, the more Australian tourism can build on its international marketing exposure and grow.

The 'best ever' Olympic Games in Sydney rewarded Australia with unprecedented positive publicity around the world, both as a sporting nation and as a desirable destination for international tourists. The Olympics were also promoted as the 'Green Games', which enabled Australian industry to showcase best practice in a range of technologies and services that reduced waste, saved energy, remediated contaminated land and provided habitat for endangered species.

Australia derives similar market exposure by hosting other international sporting events, such as the Formula 1 Grand Prix, the Rugby World Cup and soccer, cricket and other sporting tours. The Sydney to Hobart yacht race is an example of an event which has a very high international profile and draws a significant number of tourists to both Sydney and Hobart.

Even Defence can generate inbound tourism through its high profile conferences, defence industry trade exhibitions and a steady stream of defence-related international visitors. High profile arts and cultural events, such the Sydney Gay and Lesbian Mardi Gras and the Adelaide Festival of the Arts, also attract publicity for Australia in world tourism markets.

The international successes of the Australian film, television and music industries, particularly in recent years, have also boosted Australia's exposure in world markets. Australia's world-renowned educational and scientific facilities and unique natural environment combine to make Australia an attractive destination for travellers seeking research and education opportunities.

Australia's festivals-the major festivals together with regional and community festivals-attract significant numbers of visitors to their locations every year, thereby constituting key contributors to the tourism industry. For instance, performing arts festivals alone generated income of $103m in 1999-2000. Funding of events Governments at all levels contribute to projects or events that promote tourism.

These investments are in addition to marketing funding allocated to the Australian Tourist Commission, and State and Territory Tourism Commissions. The Commonwealth tends to assist in funding of events that are of national significance. For example, the Sydney 2000 Olympic and Paralympic Games received a Commonwealth contribution of around $660 million in a combination of direct funding, concessions and other costs absorbed by agencies.

Market needs

Adapting to changes in consumer tastes and capturing market share presents significant challenges for the tourism industry. Increasingly, consumers are confronted with new and innovative products and services that compete vigorously for their share of consumption spending. For example, the rapid growth in share of consumer spending on information and communications technology represents a challenge for all other industries, including tourism.

In Australia, the last decade has seen changes in the structure of the workforce, characterised by greater numbers of self-employed individuals and temporary and part-time employees making up an increasing share of the labour force. Those in full-time employment are working longer hours with less time available for leisure, leading to 'time poverty'. These trends are expected to continue over the next decade.

The challenge confronting the tourism industry will be to grow the tourism market, both internationally and domestically, and to develop new and innovative tourism products targeted to meet the needs of an increasingly time poor and discerning clientele. The ageing of Australia's population also presents a challenge for the tourism industry, including ensuring tourism product is accessible.

Increasingly, tourism operators are tailoring product to meet individual needs, and are offering short stay holiday options to complement traditional peak period long holiday options. Tourism businesses are also increasingly utilising the Internet, as a means of communicating directly with customers, rather than relying on traditional forms of marketing and advertising.

International tourist expectations pose special challenges for the industry in understanding and meeting the needs of visitors with different languages and from different cultural backgrounds. Further developing the skill base of the industry in this area will be particularly important if Australia is to fully capitalise on inbound tourism opportunities, especially from other countries in the Asia-Pacific region.

Government and industry agree that national accreditation schemes are a key vehicle for informing and encouraging operators towards world's best practice. Accreditation also provides local and international visitors and travel wholesalers with greater confidence in product quality. To be effective, accreditation schemes need critical mass and credibility to be well respected.

The Australian Tourism Accreditation Association has developed a national accreditation framework for the tourism industry, to enhance quality in management, business systems and service. Largely designed by the industry itself, the framework establishes a practical benchmark for operators. A distinctive 'tick-on-a-star' logo, to be displayed by accredited operators, signifies compliance with the framework and assures consumers that they are dealing with a committed operator.

Accreditation systems are also in operation or are being developed in a range of industry sectors, including the inbound tourism sector and the ecotourism sector, and among tour guides, outdoor recreation leaders, and Indigenous tourism operators. While many of these systems are developing independently of each other, there is support from a variety of industry sectors to ensure that, over the longer term, business accreditation systems across the industry will be embedded within, or aligned with, the single national tourism accreditation framework.

While accreditation schemes can be utilised as a means of generating competitive advantage, it is important that the net cost of adopting accreditation not be excessive, as this would impede take-up or result in unnecessarily high prices for consumers. As markets become more sophisticated, it may be that commercial considerations become more important in influencing firms towards best practice.

Visitor safety is an essential element of the operations of any tourism business and features highly in State, Territory and local government regulations as well as in business accreditation systems.

Innovation, including research and development, is widely recognised as being a major driver of economic growth. Significant Commonwealth assistance is provided in the form of tax concessions and grants for research and development.The Government has provided $100 million, under its $3 billion Innovation Action Plan, Backing Australia's Ability, to support a range of collaborative projects, including assisting Australian industry to access new technologies.

The tourism industry is only a minor beneficiary of these programs. This might be in part due to the service nature of tourism, which implies that little intellectual property in the form of patents is generated, or to a lack of knowledge about available government assistance. The economic argument advanced for providing government assistance to research activity arises from its high risk and uncertain nature, although, in reality, research in the tourism sector is probably no more high risk than in any other sector.

The potentially large external benefits to the community, and the difficulty faced by investors in appropriating the full commercial return from research when others can benefit without paying-the 'free rider' problem-is also an issue. There could be significant potential for tourism to increase its level of involvement in research and development-for example, through collaborative ventures in areas such as energy efficiency, waste disposal and construction. There could also be opportunities for further commercialisation of tourism research products and services, especially for export markets.

There are also opportunities for the tourism industry to participate in research partnerships which minimises risk to tourist, such as developing antivenom for the Irukandji jellyfish. Tourism's success is heavily dependent on its distribution channels, which link tour operators to travel agents, accommodation providers to transport operators, and so on.

Traditional distribution systems are being exposed to new competition from the use of new technology, such as online booking suites, which potentially render some service providers redundant.This process of disintermediation (or removal of a link in a traditional supply chain) is having a significant impact on the structure of the industry, globally as well as in Australia, particularly for the travel agency sector.

Global supply chains link suppliers of goods and services which transcend country boundaries. Within the tourism industry, links to international global supply chains are strongest for the travel agency, large hotels, and aviation sectors. The use of the Internet to bypass traditional methods of sourcing supply is becoming increasingly popular among suppliers, who see its ability to help them reduce costs, remain competitive and maximise their access to potential customers.

There are significant opportunities for smaller tourism businesses in generating linkages with global supply chains, but also significant inhibitors, such as prohibitive cost or lack of international profile. Overall, however, the Internet has the potential to assist such smaller players to overcome what once were insurmountable obstacles.

With rapid advances in technology, changing consumer preferences and pressures on industries to minimise cost, substantial changes in the travel distribution channels, over the next decade, are inevitable. Australia's ability to deal with these changes, including an appreciation of their implications, will have a significant bearing on the international competitiveness of the tourism industry.

A range of Commonwealth Government assistance programs is available to the tourism industry. This includes various programs to assist the development of regional and rural Australia, such as the Regional Assistance Programme, and the Regional Solutions Programme,the Regional Tourism Programme,Networking the Nation and the Export Market Development Grants Scheme.

The Commonwealth Government's $115 million Stronger Regions Programme, including the Sustainable Regions Programme, is aimed at helping regional, rural and remote communities to build their capacities to identify and implement development opportunities. The Government has also committed $163 million to improving rural and regional telecommunications and Internet services.

The Government's Regional Tourism Programme provides more targeted assistance to help businesses and other organisations to develop quality tourism products in regional Australia. An additional $8 million has been committed to the programme over the next four years. The Government has also committed funding for a range of tourism projects across Australia involving expenditure of around $14 million.

The Commonwealth Government has also committed $15 million over four years to enhance the Bass Strait Passenger Vehicle Equalisation Scheme, and has extended the diesel fuel rebate scheme to include small retail/hospitality businesses that produce their own electricity from diesel, at a cost of around $80 million over four years.

The Export Market Development Grants Scheme assists Australian companies to develop export markets. Around $150 million is being provided under the scheme in 2001-02. On average tourism receives just under 20 per cent of all grant money, which exceeds its share of total exports. Recent enhancements to this scheme have significantly increased the program's benefit to the tourism sector.

Eligible tourism providers can apply for a partial reimbursement on a broad range of expenditure, including overseas representatives and export consultants, market visits, free samples, trade fairs, seminars, in-store promotions, promotional literature and advertising, as well as bringing overseas buyers to Australia.

Tourism services expertise

Tourism services expertise is a growing segment of the tourism industry. The Australian tourism industry demonstrates best practice, leadership, high level expertise and innovation in a range of tourism related services including tourism forecasting, research, accreditation and infrastructure development and management.

For example, Australian businesses already export a number of tourism training products and services, including hotel management training. However, there are significant opportunities to increase exports in services expertise, particularly in the Asia-Pacific region, where many countries are seeking to develop their tourism sectors as engines for economic growth. Currently, there are no official measures of levels of tourism services expertise exports.

Consumers demand high quality goods and services at competitive prices. Investors expect performance and growth from their investments. The challenge for the tourism industry and its stakeholders, including governments, is to deliver positive outcomes in an increasingly globally competitive, ever changing, and technologically innovative marketplace. Meeting this challenge will require a concerted approach to risk management.

The organisations that manage risks effectively will be better placed to realise or exceed their objectives. They will be more able to identify and exploit opportunities, manage the risks that could affect achieving their objectives, make good decisions quickly, and respond and adapt to unexpected events. Successful organisations will also take calculated risks to achieve their objectives.

For the tourism industry as a whole, the more organisations that successfully manage risk, the more likely it is that the industry will perform in a way that will maximise the achievement of longer-term objectives or targets. A rigorous approach to risk management involves accurately assessing the operating environment, identifying and assessing risks and opportunities, designing strategies for managing risk and implementing risk management strategies.

In recent times, the tourism industry has weathered a number of significant events that have impacted significantly on the operations and profitability of many businesses throughout the industry.

Strategies for management

Categories of risks need to be identified before management strategies can be designed and implemented. Some examples of risk categories that could apply to tourism include: international market and currency risks, domestic market risks, infrastructure and transport risks, natural disaster and environmental risks, and business and commercial risks.

Greater internationalisation of Australia's economy and tourism market will bring higher exposure for tourism to international developments. The impact of the Gulf War in the early 1990s and, more recently, the impact of the events of 11 September 2001, each highlighted the importance of stakeholders having in place mechanisms to manage such risks.

In both cases, the inbound tourism sector, tourism marketing bodies and wider industry participants throughout the industry adjusted their marketing strategies and products on offer to respond to marked global downturns. The position of the Australian dollar against major currencies is also a key risk factor, with the devaluation which has taken place in recent times increasing the cost of marketing Australia overseas, but generally improving the competitiveness of Australia as a tourist destination.

While domestic tourism is forecast to continue to account for the bulk of tourism spending, international tourism is forecast to grow faster than domestic tourism. This has the potential to lead to a higher market share for international tourism in the Australian market. This will challenge the industry to become more responsive to international tourist needs and to place even more emphasis on becoming integrated into international markets as a means of minimising the risks associated with any downturn in domestic demand.

Similar strategies are needed to minimise risks associated with the operation of other key tourism infrastructure and transport modes, including improving the flexibility of the industry to deploy and utilise other transport modes when needed.

Bushfires which occurred close to many tourism destinations in regional New South Wales at the peak of the recent tourist holiday season highlighted the vulnerability of tourism operators who work in or close to parks and forests. For example, tourism in the Shoalhaven region of New South Wales has traditionally received 30 per cent of its business in the month after Christmas, which coincides with the peak of the bushfire season.

The risks associated with incursions by serious exotic plant, animal or marine or human diseases have been highlighted in recent times in the UK and Europe by the impact of outbreaks of foot and mouth disease and bovine spongiform encephalitis (BSE). Knowledge of human health risks, especially in the more remote of tropical areas of Australia is also an important factor for tourism operators and an integral element of ensuring visitor safety.

Within the marine tourism sector, industry and governments recently cooperated to control an outbreak of crown-of-thorns starfish which, if left unchecked, could have resulted in serious damage to coral in areas important for tourism. In addition, seasonal population increases in jellyfish, including the irukandji and the box jellyfish found in northern Australian waters, can involve significant risk for travellers involved in marine activities in these regions.

Marine tourism operators require preventive strategies to minimise risk. More generally, the tourism industry is heavily reliant on favourable weather conditions and needs to have contingency plans in place to cope with the unexpected. Planners and parks managers have a shared interest in conserving and protecting Australia's natural resources.

Having effective risk management strategies in place helps ensure the sustainability of both the resources and the businesses that depend on them. Adequately planning for business and commercial risks is as important for tourism businesses as it is for businesses generally. A prerequisite for good planning is having in place a realistic business plan embracing all the elements of good management. These relate to how the business approaches key strategic and operational issues-for example, product development, marketing, customer service, human and financial resource management, use of technology, and legal, safety and environmental management.

Many businesses seek to minimise business and commercial risk by diversifying tourism product and forming strategic alliances with related parts of the industry in cases where there is high level of interdependence. The adoption of such strategies helps to minimise over-reliance on narrow or specialised segments of the market and ensures the capacity for businesses to adjust to changing circumstances among suppliers or complementary businesses.

More broadly, the tourism industry's move towards business accreditation, both for the industry as a whole and for individual key sectors, is a positive and practical example of how businesses are moving to minimise business and commercial risks. It is also important to recognise that the industry operates within a complex regulatory environment governed by Commonwealth, State, Territory and Local governments.

Public liability insurance has become a major issue right across the tourism industry, including among airlines, rental car and other transport operators, hotels, restaurants and accommodation providers, tour operators, events organisers, horse riding schools, and adventure tourism operators. The recent rapid increase in public liability premiums and difficulties gaining access to cover are causing considerable concern for businesses-particularly small operators.

There are claims that increased premiums are causing financial hardship to operators while some operators are unable to get any cover at all. Lack of insurance cover is placing both operators and consumers at risk and, in some cases, preventing businesses from operating. While there is an ongoing debate about the causes of rising insurance premiums, few would disagree that the issue needs to be resolved as a matter of priority. Unless the issue can be resolved urgently, it has the potential to affect tourism's viability in the longer term as well as consumer confidence in the industry.

The Commonwealth, State and Territory governments are addressing a range of issues raised by industry and voluntary organisations to alleviate the impact of public liability premium increases on businesses and the community. Various possible measures have been put forward, including pooling arrangements to give small businesses greater bargaining power, caps or limitations on public liability claims, education and training for small businesses in risk management and ways to reduce the number of accidents.

The Travel Compensation Fund is both a tool for protecting consumers against financial failures of licensed travel agents, and an important element in the licensing of travel agents. Under State and Australian Capital Territory government legislation, travel agents are required to be members of the Travel Compensation Fund in order to obtain a licence. The collapse of Ansett and related companies last year has placed enormous financial pressure on Travel Compensation Fund's reserves.

This in turn has significant implications for the travel agent sector, as travel agents are the primary contributors to the Fund. Strategies for managing risk tend to fall into one of four broad categories, depending on the likely frequency of risks occurring and their severity of impact.

Risk management strategies adopted by businesses generally include avoiding, transferring, mitigating or accepting risk.If the risk associated with an opportunity is too high relative to the potential reward, it may be appropriate to drop the activity. An example would be an underwater dive operator abandoning a dive because the weather conditions are judged to be too dangerous.

Alternatively, the risk of losses can be reduced by transferring risk to third parties, for example, through insuring, outsourcing or establishing strategic alliances. If the frequency of risk occurrence and likely severity is low, many organisations tend to simply accept the risk. An example would be for a bushwalking tour guide to simply accept the risk of being sued for injury.

5

New Threats

The combined effect of a prolonged lack of economic dynamism in the world; safety concerns in view of recent security events, and hostilities in the Middle East; and the Severe Acute Respiratory Syndrome (SARS) have caused a new downturn in the travel and tourism industry that started in March 2003.

The impact of SARS, if it is not contained soon, has the potential to profoundly change the lifestyles of large populations far beyond their travel and tourism behaviour. It might affect all of the world's service industries, in particular, those which involve the ability of people to get close to each other such as on public transport and in shopping areas.

Since methods of transmitting the virus responsible for SARS are not completely known yet, people may start to avoid nonessential activities that involve personal contact with others.

Travelling, shopping and dining out are being replaced by telephone or internet contacts which include orders for home delivery of grocery and prepared food. The impact on the economy could be a multiple of the effect that SARS presently has on tourism, as it would affect residents alike. In particular, the impact on employment would be devastating, as large portions of the services sectors affected are in the hands of labour intensive small and medium sized enterprises.

The worldwide travel and tourism industry is threatened by a crisis much deeper than the slump it has suffered in 2001-2002. If the situation does not improve soon, it is estimated that by May 2003, no less than 5 million jobs may be lost in the worldwide travel and tourism industry. This represents over 6 per cent of the industry's total employment.

Taken together, all job losses from the crisis of the travel and tourism industry has been suffering since 2001 would represent 14 per cent of all jobs in the industry or one in seven. The travel and tourism industry represents over 4 per cent of GDP and over 3 per cent of employment worldwide. If indirect effects are calculated in, its portion rises as high as 11 and 8 per cent respectively. Direct employment in the industry's enterprises already amounts to about 80 million jobs.

In certain tourism-oriented countries, the travel and tourism industry accounts for more than ten per cent of direct jobs, such as Spain or the Caribbean. It is certainly the most important employer worldwide after agriculture and public services. The travel and tourism industry and its suppliers together are estimated to provide close to 200 million jobs globally, or one in every thirteen.

As a rule of thumb, one direct job in the travel and tourism industry generates employment in up to two jobs for the industry's suppliers. The slump comes after a strong global economy had propelled an international tourism boom in the late 1990's. In the peak year 2000 alone, the number of international trips increased by a record 4.5 per cent from the year before.

In the year 2001 the industry suffered disastrous effects from the events of 11 September and declined by around 1 per cent on an annual basis. Although tourism demand has traditionally bounced back one year after any crisis motivated by security problems, it did not grow significantly, if at all, during 2002. This is measured by the performance data of the hotel industry, tour operators and airlines in spite of an increase in travelling across international borders recorded by the World Tourism Organization (WTO).

In early 2003, the travel and tourism industry developed some optimism after it had been suffering an economic downturn which started in 2001 and worsened after the events of 11 September that year. It grew very little during 2002 and was stagnate in the last quarter due to security incidents in Djerba, Bali and Mombasa. The optimism dampened as early as March by a general reluctance to travel in view of the hostilities in the Middle East.

The Asian and Pacific region experienced few effects until it was exposed to new fears coming from a new disease. Business travel, which is suffering the most, generates far more than half of the hotel industry's profits as business travellers roughly spend twice as much money compared to leisure tourists. The sub-sector has been suffering severely since 2001 due to the general economic downturn.

More and more companies are now deferring business travel and are relying on supplementary methods of communication such as video-conferencing and other electronic means. New habits of communication are feared to eventually replace travelling even when things return to normal.

This would have a devastating long-term effect on the hotel and airline industries, as video conferencing could cost airlines between 5 and 10 per cent of their bookings over the next 18 months. The recently booming "meeting, incentive, conference and exhibition" business, known as MICE, is the main victim. Revenues from business travel in Asia represent a fifth of the $250 billion global business travel industry and will fall by about 5% this year. That compares with double-digit growth in each of the past four years.

Three categories of locations can be distinguished by the degrees of impact in accordance with either being affected directly or indirectly by SARS, or by the general economic and political insecurity and continuously weak economy. Countries significantly impacted on by SARS are China; Hong Kong, China; Singapore; Taiwan, China; and Viet Nam.

The second category includes the rest of South East Asia and the Pacific while the rest of the world with a few exceptions makes up the third. Rough estimates indicate that since March 2003 the travel and tourism business lost at least one third of its activities in the locations directly affected by SARS. These are Hong Kong, China; the Guangdong province of China; Taiwan, China; Singapore; and Viet Nam.

In other South East Asian countries, the immediate loss is about one third, but may be about 15 per cent in the long run. In most of the rest of the world the industry is estimated to lose about 5 per cent this year instead of growing at the rate of one or two per cent expected earlier.

The Asian and Pacific region suffered less from the crisis in tourism of the years 2001 and 2002 than other parts of the world. Growth was largely due to fast growing intra-regional tourism from markets such as Indonesia, Malaysia, Singapore and the booming Chinese market, which also comprises Hong Kong, China. Even after the security incident in Bali last October, the impact seemed to affect international travel to Bali only, especially from Australia. Bali partly managed to fill the gap by attracting local budget travelers from Indonesia and neighbouring countries.

Amongst Indonesia's annual 5 million foreign visitors, 4 million are from the ASEAN countries, Japan, the Republic of Korea and China, leaving only 20 per cent of international arrivals to Australia, New Zealand and long haul tourism. Domestic tourism is increasing in Indonesia, but international visitors spend on average 12 times more money during a trip.

Intra-regional tourism benefited the industry with two-digit annual growth rates in January and February regardless of the delicate geopolitical situation. Prospects were good for the year, as the impact of Middle East violence on Asian and Pacific tourism was not expected to affect the region in its peak season June-September. However since March 2003, the situation has dramatically changed due to SARS.

Long haul travel activities are being particularly affected. Some U.S. carriers have reported that overseas bookings have plummeted 30% to 40% in April from year-ago levels. Traffic to Asia in particular dropped by 25 per cent since December which was mainly due to SARS as it was only off about 5 percent in early March. BA carried 27 per cent fewer people on its scheduled services to the Asia-Pacific region in April than the same month last year.

Some hotels and airlines serving the directly affected locations are down to no more than 30 per cent of their usual business. A bus company in Singapore reported that business is down to ten per cent of their usual and an outbound travel agency in Taiwan, China, reported 80 per cent cancellations. Some shopkeepers in Hong Kong, China, reported not seeing a single customer for several days.

In countries directly affected, not including China, the travel and tourism industry provides about one million jobs, representing between 2.0 and 3.5 per cent of the total number of jobs. Considering all employment dependent on travel and tourism, the total is about three million jobs or between 5.4 and 9.9 per cent according to the country.

China is a special case due to its size. Whilst only one province is affected directly, the travel and tourism industry of the whole country may be affected soon. Over 15 million jobs or 2.1 per cent of all jobs are provided by China's travel and tourism industry directly, and as many as 52 million or 7.2 per cent of total employment including indirect jobs.

The core countries affected by SARS have been suffering from high ratios of cancellations in leisure travel as well as in business travel and congresses. Tourist arrivals to Hong Kong, China, slumped by some 30 per cent in the last week of March alone, and likewise,

30 per cent of flights from there were cancelled in March and early April. The occupancy rate at some of the most fashionable hotels in Hong Kong, China, was down to just 14 per cent reportedly due to the fact people could not go home.

In general, the hotel occupancy in Hong Kong, China, dropped to single-digit rates. It is estimated that Hong Kong, China, will continue to lose 6 per cent of GDP as long as the outbreak lasts. According to IATA, airlines have reduced a large percentage of flights to the region as tourist bookings have fallen by about 80 per cent impacting overall air travel to areas such as Hong Kong, China, by 30 to 40 percent.

Regional airlines still in the process of recovering from the 2001 slump, have been among the first to send out an SOS, reporting that up to 50 per cent of their flights have been suspended. Cathay Pacific (Hong Kong, China) warned that it may have to ground its entire fleet with passenger numbers predicted to fall to 20 percent of normal levels by May 2003. In general, the hotel occupancy rates in the affected locations are estimated to be down by over 30 per cent and are estimated to be below the break-even point which obliges the management to cut costs drastically.

In Vietnam, hotel occupation dropped from as high as 98 per cent to a level of only 40 per cent. In the longer term, hotel occupation rates in the affected locations may stabilize with a loss of 15 per cent. Hong Kong, China, and Singapore were amongst the poorest hotel performers in March as compared to the same period the year before, with revenue per available room falling 16.8 percent and 15.4 percent respectively. Hotels across Asia experienced a 4.6 percent decline.

The Singapore Tourism Board's (STB) latest weekly report showed that visitor arrivals to Singapore plunged by 61 per cent in the first thirteen days of April, as compared to the same period a year ago. Hotel occupancy rates fell to 20-30 per cent from normal levels of at least 70 per cent. The Singapore Retailers Association reported that sales could fall by as much as 75 per cent for some firms. Declines for general stores perhaps range between 20 and 40 per cent.

Singapore, which like Hong Kong, China, relies heavily on tourism and its role as a regional transport hub, has cut its economic growth target to 0.5-2.5 per cent this year from 2.0-5.0 per cent due to the impact of SARS. The late disclosure by the Chinese authorities of the SARS outbreak has created additional concern amongst travelers. The Grand Hyatt in Shanghai reports an occupancy rate of about 30 percent compared to last year in mid-April when the hotel was nearly full.

Four major hotels in China's biggest city were closing for up to three months due to a lack of guests. Prospects are that the tourism business in all of China may be affected soon. For example, Beijing and the Shanxi province came to the limelight when the World Health Organization recommended the postponement of unnecessary travel there, as the organization had done earlier for Guangdong province and Hong Kong, China, and later also for the provinces of Tianjin and Inner Mongolia (as well as Taipei).

China's inbound tourism industry brought in 20.4 billion dollars in foreign currency last year. Chinese tourism industry analysts estimate that tourist income may fall at least 40 percent this year. In other Southern and South Eastern countries the travel and tourism industry is affected by SARS because of direct flight connections to indexed locations. These countries are also affected by the notoriously weak geographical knowledge on the world's tourism markets which has resulted in a large de-facto "quarantine area" in South East Asia and Oceania comprising important tourism countries such as Thailand, Indonesia, and the Philippines as well as neighboring Australia and New Zealand.

The travel and tourism industry in Indonesia, Philippines, and Thailand alone means over 5 million direct jobs and a total of over 12 million jobs including those in other industries depending on travel and tourism. Their share in total employment is as high as 11 and 12 percent in Thailand and the Philippines respectively, i.e. one in nine jobs is in danger when travel and tourism slumps, and 6 per cent in Indonesia.

Direct employment in the industry represents as much as 2.4 percent of total employment in Indonesia, 4.1 and 5.7 per cent in the Philippines and Thailand respectively. In Indonesia, foreign arrivals are down about 15 percent for Jakarta and 20 percent for Bali airport. Flights arriving from Singapore fell by about 30 per cent due to the outbreak of SARS in that country. Indonesian hoteliers have seen occupancy rates quickly tumble by about 10 per cent.

Thailand, one of Asia's most tourist-dependent economies, earned over USD 8 billion from tourism last year. Thai Hotels are currently experiencing cancellation rates of 5 to 10 per cent. According to the Tourism Authority of Thailand, which predicted a 40 per cent drop in foreign visitors coming to Thailand between April and June, About 50,000 visits were cancelled for the period between April and June 2003.

Five-star hotels in Bangkok are expecting an occupation rate of no more than 30 per cent for April 2003. April falls in the lean season, but in April 2002, the occupancy rate was still 50 per cent. Arrivals to Cambodia fell by 22 per cent in March and are frustrating expectations to reach the one-million line this year, which would have brought a 25 per cent increase over last year's 800,000 visitors. Cambodia had reported a 17% one-year increase in arrivals in January and 33% in February.

The Philippines remained moderately affected so far, with a drop of foreign arrivals by 4 percent in the first quarter as compared to the first quarter 2002, in spite of a 13 per cent growth in January over last December. Similar to other visitors, South East Asian finance ministers postponed their trip to Manila where their annual summit was to be held, although the ASEAN labour ministers' meeting took place in West Nusa Tenggara.

Malaysia, on the other hand, is heavily affected, with airline bookings down by 40 per cent and hotel occupancy rates by as much as 30 per cent. Industry officials say some hotels are seeing occupancy rates dip as low as 30 per cent after cancellations not only from tourists but also due to postponements of corporate events and shows.

In Korea, arrivals of foreign air travelers dropped by almost 50 per cent last month compared to April 2002. Australia and New Zealand are affected by SARS, as far as the markets on the northern hemisphere are concerned, due to their geographical closeness to the core countries hit by SARS. As both countries are considering closing their borders for travelers from those locations, arrivals through places like Singapore or Hong Kong, China, would also be excluded.

Already at present, the Australian Hotels Association has confirmed bookings are on the decline with occupancy falling by between 20 and 30 per cent and tour operators informed bookings of foreign visitors for May are down 30 per cent and for June 20 per cent as compared to the same period last year. In February, cancellations were highest from the United States, the United Kingdom, Italy, France, Germany and the Netherlands, but since news of the SARS virus hit the headlines, Asian tourists have also started canceling.

SARS is expected to cost New Zealand about 20,000 visits by East Asian tourists and around $60.7 million a month at its present level. The Tourism Board predicts a 15 per cent decline in the number of Asian visitors in 2003 because of the SARS infection scare. In other parts of the world, the 2001-02 crisis of the travel and tourism industry continues due to SARS, but hostilities in the Middle East and the state of the overall economy play the predominant role.

Instead of growing by between 1 and 2 percent or more as forecasted by several sources, the worldwide travel and tourism industry is facing cancellations and a low level of reservations for the northern summer, as well as a continuous decline of business travel. The loss of income is estimated to amount in average to 5 per cent for the world without South East Asia, China and Oceania.

The average current loss of income for the whole world is estimated to amount to 7 per cent. In the United States, hotel occupancy rates have dropped to an average of 60 per cent in the first quarter 2003 from 63 per cent over the last year according to the Travel Industry Association. They are forecast to run at about 59 per cent occupancy rate this year, whilst 65 per cent is usual in good years.

As the break-even point is as low as about 55 per cent, the hotel sector in general in the United States continues being profitable due to rigorous cost cuts in the recent past and a rational financial structure. However, PricewaterhouseCoopers projects a 7 per cent drop in the sector's earnings this year to $15 billion from $16.1 billion in 2002. Hotel loan delinquencies are at their highest level since the early 1990's.

The negative outlooks for 2003 follow the release of 2002 data by the United States Department of Commerce indicating that the number of international visitors declined 7 percent compared to 2001. The demand for hotel rooms in the United States has never been weaker than at present; since before the war in Iraq and the development of SARS most companies were only travelling on business trips deemed essential. This is a significant blow to the industry since at least three-quarters of the hotel sector's profits come from business travelers.

The number of business trips this spring is expected to fall 2.5 per cent from the spring of 2002 and 13 per cent from spring 2001, according to the Travel Industry Association. A quick recovery is not likely. The Mexican tourist industry reported a 17.1 per cent slide in reservations since the beginning of the war in Iraq. More than 3.5 million travelers have called off their trips to the country, which calculates into losses of up to USD 700 million in revenues or 9 per cent of the tourism sector's annual hard currency income.

International travel to France had rebounded in the past year but is currently levelling down. In Germany, the hotel federation announced that the industry might have to cut as many as 10,000 jobs. Hotel bookings in Rome, Florence and Venice, Italy, ordinarily throbbing in springtime with art lovers and business travellers, were reported to be down by half compared with last year.

In Paris, occupancy rates at four-star hotels dropped 25 percent by March 25. The drop was mainly attributed to the absence of Americans, who accounted last year for 19 per cent of all foreign visitors to Paris. Second to the Japanese at USD 652,.8 Americans usually spend more in Paris, an average of USD 328 a day, compared to USD 133 by British tourists, and USD 78 for Germans.

In Turkey, foreign tour operators cancelled between 15 and 40 per cent of reservations. Despite being 1,000 kilometres from Iraq, congresses in Istanbul are being postponed. This affects Turkey's goal to attract 15 million tourists and earn USD 11 billion from tourism this year. There is still hope for tourism to recover as Europeans typically visit Turkey in summer.

The present job losses come after the industry already lost an estimated six and a half million jobs before the recent events such as SARS and the hostilities in the Middle East. The compounded loss of eleven and a half million jobs over the 2001-2003 crisis relates to an estimated total of about 80 million jobs in the industry, and represents a loss of one in every jobs. The capacity of the travel and tourism industry to create employment seems to be severely damaged by the recent events.

Additional factors may need to be considered if the slump continues. The longer the loss of travel and tourism activities lasts, the possibility exists that more jobs will be eliminated entirely. The reductions in working hours and manpower tend to become permanent, as the missing labour force is made up for by new working methods such as increased versatility. Remaining core staff is induced to acquire additional skills and also accept more flexible working hours.

A hotel and resort company in the United States and Canada reported having eliminated 15 percent of 38,500 jobs and having trained many of the remaining employees to handle multiple tasks. For example, a front-desk person may also take phone reservations and an administrative person in the back office will help check people in during busy times. Modernization of working methods, working relationships and indeed enterprise structures may thus take a sudden leap forward and leave behind a number of employees with reduced or no income.

The loss of employment affects the socially weaker and lesser skilled staff members, as well as part time workers including high proportions of women, migrant workers and young workers. They risk permanently losing income and jobs as long as the industry does not return to substantial growth rates. The social effect is worse as it severely impacts on those workers who have difficulty finding alternative jobs due to lower skills levels.

If indirect effects of the crisis are counted in, that is, jobs which are lost in industries that provide inputs to the travel and tourism industry, the estimated loss amounts to over 13 million jobs worldwide. This is to be added to at least the same impact of indirect effects that was already produced by the crisis since 2001. As a rule of thumb, one direct job in the travel and tourism industry generates as an indirect effect, two additional jobs in related industries.

It should be considered, however, that industries providing inputs to the travel and tourism industry will suffer from downturns in this sector with some time lag only, and employment may not be reduced as quickly as in the sector concerned directly. Companies of the travel and tourism sector report on measures aiming at rapid cost cutting and in some cases downsizing to reduce over-capacities acquired in the 1990's.

In Germany, the world leader in tour operating, TUI, recently announced a million cost-cutting programme for 2004, and the possible loss of 2,000 jobs. In the course of the crisis in the travel and tourism industry, representative bodies of the industry and government authorities have been trying in many countries to develop measures to mitigate the effects, at least in the short run.

Tourism crisis plans are being developed and government relief measures such as tax breaks are being asked for, although with limited success due to high deficits in government accounts from the economic downturn since 2001. Positive examples of private-public partnerships have been developed to promote the tourism destination. In some cases such as Canada, Indonesia, Australia, and others, particular efforts are being made to target closer markets in view of slumping long haul international arrivals.

Benefit of Tourism

The benefits of tourism expenditure accrue first to

regional economies, then flow-on across the national economy. Tourist spending is income for local communities. To the extent that local businesses 'import' materials and rely on other regions to supply inputs, the rest of the economy benefits. It is also important to acknowledge that there are costs associated with tourism. These can be a local or national concern, or both. As well as tangible costs such as, say, localised price increases, tourism can impose costs on a community that are harder to measure.

Examples of these intangible costs are increased traffic congestion or crowding and environmental impacts at popular sites. If economic development is augmented by tourism growth, net of associated costs, the tourism industry can generate a compound benefit across regions or the entire nation. However, net benefits at a national level only result if either or both of the following circumstances prevail: there is under utilisation of resources, and expansion of the tourism industry does not give rise to increased production costs; and tourism is a more profitable activity than other industries presently using resources and re-allocation of resources to tourism increases the value of output.

As tourism is an amalgam of many other industries, the expenditure of tourists has direct impacts on many businesses, including: hospitality businesses such as hotels, restaurants and cafes; travel and transport related businesses such as travel agents and transport operators; international travel businesses such as airlines and shipping agents; and recreational and service industries such as dive tours and charter boat services.

The most effective means of measuring the size of tourism is by gathering data on what tourists spend. The

World Tourism Organisation (WTO) reported that international tourists spent US$372 billion for calendar year 1995 and the industry contributed 1.3 per cent to world gross domestic product (GDP).

According to the International Visitor Survey (IVS) in the year ending September 1995, 3.3 million inbound tourists aged 15 years and over stayed for an average of 24 nights and spent about $1935 each within Australia (BTR 1996). This amounted to total expenditure by inbound visitors in Australia of $6.47 billion or about 1.5 per cent of GDP for that year. Generally tourism data are collected for calendar years.

Data from the WTO for tourism receipts represents preliminary estimates for 1995. The total is computed on the basis of data supplied by individual countries and does not include airfares. GDP equals the market value of all final goods and services produced in an economy during a given time period (usually a year).

The fact that many inbound tourists buy packages (airfares, accommodation, tours etc.) in their country of origin makes it difficult to present an accurate picture of expenditure patterns in Australia. Package tour purchase prices generally include a large proportion of the total cost of accommodation. Indeed tourists who travel on package tours generally have low expenditure figures within Australia, having purchased the majority of their accommodation - as well as airfares and transfers - in the package price.

Noting the difficulties in estimating what is spent on Australian tourism goods and services due to the payment overseas for many of these items, the available data indicate that average total expenditure by inbound visitors in Australia has decreased in real terms from 1990 to 1995. However, average expenditure per night has increased in real terms.

Table 1 presents a summary of the components of tourism expenditure within Australia by inbound tourists during the year to September 1995. It excludes package travel. Expenditure on food, drink and accommodation within Australia represented approximately 34 per cent of total purchases per visit in the year ending September 1995, generating expenditure of $659 per person.

Expenditure patterns vary according to the main reason for travel to Australia. For example, in the year to September 1995, business travellers spent $2158, holiday makers $1684 and tourists visiting friends and relatives spent $1474 per trip. In the year to September 1995, business travellers spent $1144 of their per trip expenditure on food drink and accommodation, holiday makers $525 and tourists visiting friends and relatives spent $468.

One sub-category of holiday-makers, backpackers, spent $1633 per trip on food, drink and accommodation in this period. This stems from the fact that backpackers stay in Australia much longer than other holiday-makers and, even though they use relatively inexpensive accommodation, this is more than off-set by their length of stay.

Inbound tourism expenditure also varies according to the country of origin of the tourist. Table 1 presents the average expenditure within Australia for tourists from a number of Australia's significant inbound tourism markets. The data are for the year ending September 1995. Tourists from Europe tend to spend more in

Australia than other foreign visitors. The average expenditure for tourists from Other Asia - a combined source category, not including Japan - was the next highest in absolute terms.

Table 1 Average expenditure within Australia per inbound visitor, by country of origin, year to September 1995

Region of origin	Total visitors ('000)	Average expenditure per visitor ($)	Total expenditure ($m)
Japan	730	1,494	1,091
Other Asia	924	2,334	2,157
USA and Canada	334	2,153	719
United Kingdom[a]	344	1,981	681
Other Europe	367	2,587	949
New Zealand	474	1,194	566
Other Countries	171	1,807	308
All regions	3,344	1,935	6,471

Note: Includes all expenditure within Australia, but does not include purchases of travel packages. Includes travellers in transit, accompanying business travellers, medical reasons, employment, religious pilgrims and education. Education is the largest component of average expenditure for this group of visitors and reflects the influence of high levels of student expenditure in this category, including capital expenditure such ascars and computers. This is likely to inflate expenditure from Other Asia.

[a] Includes the Republic of Ireland.

Source: BTR 1996, p. 12

Tourists from the United States and Canada - another combined source category - also had high average expenditure. The travel preferences of tourists from various markets also influence their expenditure patterns within Australia. In particular, the high average expenditure within Australia for tourists from the United Kingdom and Europe can be partly explained by their preference for independent travel - as opposed to package travel - and their longer average duration of stay compared to Asian visitors. The relatively low average expenditure within Australia by Japanese tourists is largely explained by the short duration of their visits.

Domestic tourism expenditure

Domestic tourism expenditure has historically been the largest component of total tourism expenditure in Australia. The Domestic Tourism Expenditure Survey (DTES) conducted by the BTR in 1992 contains the most recent comprehensive estimates of domestic tourism expenditure. The DTES calculated total domestic tourism expenditure, as well as expenditure by type of trip and region.

In 1992, total domestic tourism expenditure was $28.6 billion, or 7.2 per cent of GDP, with accommodation accounting for $3.1 billion or nearly one per cent of An inclusive tour includes all of the price of airfares and some, or all, of the price of transfers, accommodation and tours taken as part of the package. Package tourists on all-inclusive tours still have some expenditure in Australia, although it is less than the expenditure of a tourist on a semi-inclusive tour.

There were 46 million domestic overnight trips with an average expenditure of $395 per trip during 1992. Average expenditure on accommodation was $101 per trip (excluding trips spent with friends and relatives), and $68 per trip if all types of trips are taken into account.

BTR estimated that total Australian expenditure on day trips in 1992 was $10.4 billion. This figure is the product of a total of 253 million day trips by Australian residents, with average expenditure being $41 per trip. There was some minor variation according to the state/territory of origin: New South Wales ($42), Victoria ($42), Queensland ($41), Northern Territory ($48), Western Australia ($44), ACT ($42), Tasmania ($34) and South Australia ($32).

On the basis of the most recent data published by the BTR, currently domestic tourism - including day trips - is considerably larger than inbound tourism in terms of expenditure. However, the rate of growth of inbound tourism is forecast to be significantly higher than the rate of growth of domestic tourism. Based on the TFC estimate of 9 per cent compound growth over the decade 1993 to 2003, inbound tourism expenditure is estimated to reach $14.5 billion (in 1993 dollars) by 2003.

Nevertheless, this would be only half of the amount of spending by domestic tourists in 1992. On this basis, in terms of expenditure, domestic tourism activity should be much greater than inbound tourism for the foreseeable future. Real inbound tourism spending has been growing at an average rate of about 10 per cent per annum. It has increased from 7 per cent of current account credits in 1981 to over 10 per cent of credits in 1994, growing more quickly than total exports.

Real domestic tourism spending grew at about 4.5 per cent per annum (in real terms) between 1982 and 1992, compared with real consumption spending growth of 3 per cent per annum over the same period. That is, domestic spending on tourism has been growing faster than other household spending. The structure of the economy has thus tended to shift towards tourism-related industries; as disposable incomes have increased, tourism expenditure has increased faster relative to other types of expenditure.

Another way of understanding the economic impact of tourism is to consider tourism's export earnings. Some participants in the inquiry, including the Commonwealth Department of Tourism (DoT), focused on the forecast growth of inbound tourism and the (export) income it generates. The Commonwealth Department of Tourism commented:

... As a destination, Australia not only competes with other tourist destinations for the business of foreign tourists, but it also competes with those destinations for the business of Australian tourists. The choice by Australian tourists between competing destinations within Australia and overseas has implications for tourism accommodation in Australia and the balance of payments. It is the balance of the flows of tourists, both inbound and outbound that is important in determining the current account outcomes.

As tourism affects many parts of the economy, it is useful to go beyond a discussion of tourism expenditure and its current account implications and include the effect of such spending on related sectors in the economy. Further, it evaluates the impact of tourism's increasing importance in the economy using a general equilibrium modelling approach.

Inbound tourism was estimated to contribute $10.5 billion to the Australian economy in 1994. This figure includes an estimate of the amount of package tour expenditure which is ultimately paid to Australian providers of hotel rooms etc. but excludes imports purchased directly by tourists. It is not directly comparable to data reported by the BTR, ABS, or TFC.

Domestic holiday tourism expenditure was estimated to contribute $14 billion to the Australian economy in 1992. Expenditure on accommodation represented about 16 per cent of this expenditure. The analysis was conducted using the ORANI model of the Australian economy. This type of analysis does not provide a forecast of the Australian economy; rather, it provides insights into the mechanisms through which the economy adapts to the modelled changes. It distinguishes the effects of a specific change in the economy from the multitude of other factors that influence economic outcomes.

Increased tourism spending affects the whole economy as suppliers. Business tourism is a business expense which is expected to vary with the general level of economic activity. Simulation results indicate that the economy-wide effects of increased tourism activity depend on the state of the economy in which these increases occur. In particular, increased tourism activity can result in an increased economy-wide demand for labour.

If this occurs when labour can be hired without significantly increasing real wages, the simulations indicate that there is a potential gain for the Australian economy. However, if real wages increase in response to the increased demand for labour, then production costs for all industries increase according to simulation results. This wage increase reduces the competitiveness of Australia's exports in world markets and results in lower levels of exports, production and income than if tourism's share of economic activity had remained unchanged.

At the same time, as the prices of Australian produced goods increase, consumers and producers are expected to switch towards cheaper imports. The impacts also depend on whether the increased tourism activity is initially associated with a net increase in economic activity over what would have occurred in the absence of the modelled changes (as with inbound tourism), or results from an increase in the share of tourism expenditure (as with domestic holiday tourism).

That is, as domestic incomes rise, expenditure on holiday tourism rises more than proportionately with income. This scenario does not provide the same opportunities for expanding production as does the net expansion of inbound tourism. Simulation results are summarised in Table 2. The first two columns show the impact of changes in inbound and domestic tourism expenditures assuming that employment is able to adjust without significantly altering real wages. The last two columns show results for identical changes in tourism expenditure, assuming that the economy is less able to supply workers to growing industries and changes in real wages occur as a result.

The percentage changes reported reflect changes in variables in addition to what they would be had the economy grown without a shift toward tourism expenditure. The greatest economic impact occurs in scenario 1, when wages are assumed not to rise in response to increased demand for labour. The simulations indicate changes modelled will implicitly be reflected in the level of business travel and are therefore accounted for in the model.

This assumes that labour is homogeneous and that it is relatively easy to switch from one occupation to another. This is a reasonable assumption if enough time is allowed for workers to be trained in the professions required by the expanding sectors of the economy that the benefits to the Australian economy result from its ability to adjust to the increased demand for inbound tourism through higher employment.

Table 2 Economy-wide impacts of a 10 per cent increase tourism demand (percentage changes)

	Employment adjusts		Wages adjust	
Macroeconomic Aggregates	Increased inbound expenditure Scenario (1)	Increased domestic expenditure Scenario (2)	Increased inbound expenditure Scenario (3)	Increased domestic expenditure Scenario (4)
Real GDP	0.34	..	0.05	-0.05
Real consumption	0.20	0.03	0.06	0.01
Export volume	1.13	0.01	0.29	-0.14
Import volume	0.41	0.04	0.32	0.02
Export prices	0.01	..	0.21	0.04
Real wages	0[a]	0[a]	0.14	0.02
Employment	0.32	0.06	0.01	..

[a] Indicates that a variable is held fixed in the simulation.
.. Percentage change is between -0.005 and +0.005.

In contrast, simulation results in scenario 3 show that when employment can not expand in response to increased demand, wages increase as labour is bid away from other sectors into the tourism sector. This increase in wages causes the costs of producing export commodities to rise. This reduces exports of non-tourism products sufficiently to counteract the initial increase in export revenues associated with increased inbound tourism spending.

Consequently, in this scenario, the rest of the economy contracts in response to the expansion of the tourism sector. The impact of reallocating domestic consumer expenditure to tourism expenditure is shown in scenarios 2 and 4 under the same labour market assumptions used for the inbound tourism scenarios.

When labour is available at the prevailing wage rate, the increased share of tourism expenditure has little economy-wide impact. Because tourism industries tend to use more labour per unit of output than the rest of the economy, employment increases slightly. In scenario 4, the combination of the lack of an expansionary effect and the upward pressure on the wage rate results in increased export prices and reduced activity.

The effect of the modelling, under all the scenarios, on industries that sell most of their output to tourists is unambiguously positive. This is especially the case for the accommodation industry; its output increases by between 2.6 and 5.5 per cent in the simulations. In scenario 1, the tourism-oriented services sector stimulates activity in the rest of the economy, promoting new employment.

In scenario 3 the stimulation is inhibited by a shortage of labour, resulting in increased costs. This increase in costs has a negative impact on agricultural and mining exports. In scenario 2, increased domestic tourism expenditure promotes new employment. The simulation results indicate potential pressures on parts of the Australian economy as tourism expenditure as a share of aggregate expenditure increases. If the growth in this share increases more quickly than does the availability of resources such as labour, this expansion can be expected to occur to the detriment of other sectors in the economy.

Alternatively, if additional resources are available, the tourism sector can expand to the benefit of the economy as a whole. In short, the economic impact of tourism will be influenced by the type of tourists and the pattern of their expenditure.

Segmentation of Tourism

An association of Canadian tourism ministries and organizations have collaborated to conduct two large scale surveys to assess the travel activities and motivators of pleasure travel among Canadians and Americans. This survey, known as the Travel Activities and Motivation Survey (TAMS), represents the comprehensive assessment of travel behavior and motivators, and provides a rich and authoritative database to develop marketing strategies and travel products to attract visitors to Canada and Ontario.

A series of analyses are being conducted using the TAMS database to explore the travel patterns of the marketplace as well as the factors which motivate travel behavior. TAMS consisted of both a telephone survey and a self-completed mailback survey. The survey was conducted in Canada and the United States between September 27, 1999 and April 16, 2000. The telephone survey was completed by 28,397 individuals in the United States and by 18,385 individuals in Canada. Respondents were selected randomly within the household.

The Touring Segmentation is intended to provide greater insight into different interests that exist within the market for various types of vacation touring activities. This information can be used to develop strategic initiatives to attract selected sectors of the market to Canada and Ontario.

The Touring Segmentation was developed using a two-stage process. In the first stage, a series of prime core segmentors were constructed to identify patterns in the day and overnight touring activities of individuals while on a trip during the past two years. These variables were submitted to a nearest centroid cluster analysis through an iterative process, to produce several possible segmentation solutions.

In total, 17 segmentation solutions were constructed and tested for their ability to identify sectors of the market with common interest in touring activities, before selecting the final segmentation solution. It is acknowledged that segmentation analyses, like all segmentation research, is partly statistical and partly artistic in nature.

While a large variety of core segmentors were developed and tested in this process, the final clustering solution selected for the Touring Segmentation was based on the following 12 core segmentors:

1. The extent to which individuals had taken day and overnight scenic bus tours of cities or the countryside
2. The extent to which individuals had taken day and overnight wine tours
3. The extent to which individuals had explored small towns/rural areas or taken scenic drives using their own vehicles
4. The extent to which individuals had taken day and overnight air, boat or train tours
5. The extent to which individuals had taken cruises on the Great Lakes or submarine cruises

6. The extent to which individuals had taken an ocean cruise
7. The extent to which the individual had sought out exploratory vacation experiences during the past two years
8. The interest exhibited in wine and cuisine while on vacation
9. The education level of the respondent
10. The household's annual income
11. The marital status of the respondent
12. Whether the individual was a member of the Youth Segment, the Family Segment, the Mature Segment or the Senior Segment based on the Demographic Lifespan Segmentation.

In the final stage of this analysis, the six identified Touring Segments were profiled using a wide variety of data from both the telephone survey and mailback survey.

Wine Tour Enthusiasts

Wine Tour Enthusiasts account for 8.7 % of Canadian travellers and 9.6 % of American travellers. They are over-represented among the Affluent Mature and Senior Couples, Affluent Young Couples and Affluent Mature Singles, and report above average household incomes and levels of education. Wine Tour Enthusiasts have travelled frequently over the past two years, both domestically and internationally. They are also more likely than the average traveller to be planning a trip in

Canada over the next two years (73% versus 68%). Moreover, they represent an important off-peak travel market since they are 25 % more likely than the typical traveller to take a trip during the low seasons.

Canadian Wine Tour Enthusiasts seem very aware of the country's main wine regions, and were more likely than the average Canadian traveller to have visited Ontario and British Columbia. However, American Wine Tour Enthusiasts were no more likely to have visited Ontario and British Columbia than the average American visitor to Canada, but were slightly more likely to have visited Quebec.

Wine Tour Enthusiasts undertake vacation travel primarily for exploration and personal indulgence. They are likely to patronize the high arts (ballet, opera), seek out natural attractions, and appear drawn to garden attractions. Satisfying their personal indulgences while on vacation trips goes beyond enjoying food and wine, and includes shopping and casino gambling. They also prefer luxury accommodations.

Wine Tour Enthusiasts participate in a wide variety of outdoor activities while on vacation including golfing, sailing, canoeing, kayaking and hiking. Along with wine tours, Wine Tour Enthusiasts showed above average interest in other touring activities, such as guided country or city tours, scenic day tours by air, and ocean cruises. Wine Tour Enthusiasts tended to consult a wide array of information sources when planning their vacations.

As such, the most efficient channels for reaching this segment are travel magazines, travel guides, direct mail travel information, and specialized trade or travel shows. Wine Tour Enthusiasts were also more likely than others to use the Internet to research and book their vacation travel. Wine Tour Enthusiasts were also more likely than the average traveller to use travel packages for both brief and longer vacations. In fact, 40 % have used travel packages for at least some of their longer vacations during the past two years.

Scenic Tour Seekers

Scenic Tour Seekers represent 8.9 % of Canadian travellers and 9.5 % of American travellers. Their levels of education and household income were lower than those of other touring travellers, and closer to those of the general population. Mature Mainstream Singles and Senior Singles were especially over-represented among the Scenic Tour Seekers.

Scenic Tour Seekers travelled less often than the average traveller, both domestically and internationally. Ontario was the most popular destination for both Canadian and American Scenic Tour Seekers, but American Tour Seekers were more likely than average to be drawn to the scenic attractions of British Columbia and Alberta.

Most Canadian Scenic Tour Seekers were planning a Canadian vacation in the next two years, although this incidence fell below the national average. American Scenic Tour Seekers were just as likely as other American vacationers to be planning a Canadian trip. Scenic Tour Seekers are most likely to seek out exploratory vacation experiences. They were less likely to have used their vacations as opportunities to seek out romance and relaxation.

Guided tours of a city or the countryside were the most preferred touring activities, and Scenic Tour Seekers exhibited little interest in other types of touring. They were also less likely to participate in outdoor activities, and showed average participation levels in most culture and entertainment activities. They were also more likely to use a motorhome or travel trailer than other travellers.

In combination, these findings suggest that "scenic touring" is the main travel pursuit of this segment. Scenic Tour Seekers were less active vacation planners than the other touring segments. They did not consult any source of information more often than the average traveller. They were below average users of the Internet, which reflects the age of this segment. However, they are above average viewers of daytime television.

Personal Explorers

Personal Explorers are the largest of the touring segments, accounting for 23.0 % of Canadian travellers and 24.2 % of American travellers. They are younger than other touring travellers, and are more likely to be employed full time. They have above average household incomes and levels of education. Affluent Young Couples and Affluent Mature and Senior Couples were especially over-represented within this segment.

The size and travel activities of the Personal Explorers make this a prime segment for Canada. Relative to average travellers, Canadian Personal Explorers were more likely to have travelled domestically and American Personal Explorers were more likely to have visited Canada during the past two years.

Moreover, both Canadian and American Personal Explorers were more likely to expect to vacation in Canada during the next two years.

Personal Explorers are also more likely to travel during all four seasons of the year than the average traveller. Personal Explorers sought out a broad range of vacation experiences during the past two years. They were especially likely to have sought out exploratory vacation experiences, and frequently use their vacations as opportunities for romance and relaxation. They were also more likely than the average traveller to have used their travel for personal indulgence, to participate in a sport or hands-on learning experience, or to socialize with family and friends.

Personal Explorers are also quite active in a number of outdoor activities including natural sightseeing, canoeing, kayaking and hiking. Their prime cultural and entertainment pursuits while travelling included shopping and dining, and visiting museums, art exhibits and historical sites. Personal Explorers tour almost exclusively by personal vehicle. With the exception of a marked interest in wine tours, they were less likely than average to embark on other types of day or overnight touring activities. Travel packages also were less often purchased by Personal Explorers than by other travellers.

Personal Explorers were not likely to choose the most luxurious vacation accommodations, but rather appear to prefer a cottages (either rented or one that they own), camping, and B&Bs. They exhibit a decided interest in nature, both in terms of the accommodations they stay in, and in the types of outdoor pursuits they participate in.

Personal Explorers consulted a wide variety of sources when researching their vacations, including travel guidebooks, travel or sportsmen's shows, newspaper or magazine ads, and material from travel information offices/auto clubs. They also were more likely than the average traveller to use the Internet for general information and to book their travel.

Exotic Tour Seekers

Exotic Tour Seekers represent 8.9 % of Canadian travellers and 9.4 % of American travellers. They are typical of touring travellers in terms of their age (average age is 45.8 years), but they report above average education levels and household incomes. Affluent Families, Mainstream Mature Couples and Mainstream Mature Singles were slightly over-represented within this segment, although Exotic Tour Seekers are less distinctive from a demographic perspective than other touring segments.

Exotic Tour Seekers find "the exotic" both domestically and overseas. They were more likely than others to visit countries beyond North America and the Caribbean (20% versus 14%), but were also more likely to travel domestically than the average traveller. Moreover, both Canadian and American Exotic Tour Seekers (86% and 47%, respectively) were more likely than the average traveller to have plans to travel in Canada over the next two years.

In the past two years, Canadian Exotic Tour Seekers were much more likely than the average traveller to have visited Quebec, while their American counterparts were much more likely to have visited British Columbia. Exotic Tour Seekers were more likely than others to seek out exploratory vacation experiences. They exhibit particular interest in natural sightseeing and visiting natural phenomena.

They also were more likely than the average traveller to have participated in vigorous physical activity outdoors when on vacation, including fitness activities, canoeing, kayaking, hiking, sailing, windsurfing and scuba diving. Exotic Tour Seekers also displayed a marked interest in visiting gardens and natural attractions as well as zoos, aquariums and planetariums, a reflection of their interest in opportunities to explore the natural world.

They were much more likely than any other travellers to have taken scenic day trips by boat, train and air. Their desire to get back to nature was also reflected in their choice of accommodations, which includes stays at lodges or cottages. Exotic Tour Seekers used a wider array of travel information sources to plan their vacations than the typical traveller. Travel and sportsmen's shows, television programs, travel information received in the mail, and printed materials from travel information offices were especially likely to be used by Exotic Tour Seekers to plan their vacations.

Travel packages oriented towards unique natural areas will likely appeal to most Exotic Tour Seekers. They were more likely than other travellers to purchase travel packages for both brief and longer vacation trips. In fact, 44 % of Exotic Tour Seekers have purchased travel packages for at least some of their longer vacations within the last two years.

Ocean Cruise Enthusiasts

Ocean Cruise Enthusiasts were the smallest of the touring segments, accounting for only 5.3 % of Canadian travellers and 8.0 % of American travellers. They have the highest household incomes of the five touring segments ($66,700), and are also the oldest. Affluent Mature and Senior Couples and Mainstream Senior Couples were especially over-represented within this segment, although Affluent Young Couples and Affluent Couples were also over-represented.

Ocean Cruise Enthusiasts are clearly drawn to southern destinations. They are three times more likely than other travellers to have visited Mexico or the Caribbean in the past two years. They were also more likely than the average traveller to have visited other international vacation destinations. Their vacation travel exhibits a clear seasonal pattern, as they were 14 % more likely to have taken a trip during the off-peak travel seasons (fall, winter and spring).

However, the Canadian travel activities of Ocean Cruise Enthusiasts were not negligible. Canadian Ocean Cruise Enthusiasts were more likely than the average traveller to visit Atlantic Canada and British Columbia during the past two years, and 70 % intended to take a trip in Canada over the next two years. American Ocean Cruise Enthusiasts parallel the average American traveller, both in terms of the incidence of trips to each Canadian province over the past two years, and in terms of their intention to visit Canada during the next two years.

Ocean Cruise Enthusiasts sought out vacation experiences that provided opportunities for personal indulgence and for exploration. Among their preferred personal indulgences, Ocean Cruise Enthusiasts were much more likely than other travellers to visit casinos and theme parks. Their preferred outdoor activities include sailing, swimming and sunbathing, viewing natural phenomena, and golfing.

Their exploratory vacation pursuits included visiting museums, art exhibits and historical sites. Ocean Cruise Enthusiasts were also more likely than the average traveller to take guided tours of cities or the countryside, and to stay in hotels and seaside resorts. Compared to other vacation travellers, Ocean Cruise Enthusiasts were more likely to use a travel agent and the Internet to plan their trips.

One-quarter of Ocean Cruise Enthusiasts have also used the Internet to book at least one trip in the past two years. Ocean Cruise Enthusiasts relied more than others on travel information received in the mail, travel ads in newspapers and magazines, and travel magazines. They were also much more likely than other travellers to purchase travel packages for their trips.

6

Consequences of New Challenges

The terrorist attacks in New York and Washington on 11 September 2001 were unprecedented in their scale and impact. The immediate response of the United States Government and the subsequent commencement of military action against the Government of Afghanistan and the terrorist network led by Osama Bin Laden hold out the prospect of an extended period of global insecurity.

The travel and tourism sector of the global economy is, by common consent, the most vulnerable of all sectors to the threat of insecurity and was immediately affected. However, because the scale of this attack and its aftermath have no precedent in the modern history of global travel and tourism, there is no historical basis for judging their probable effects.

While an examination of the effects of previous disturbances to global peace offer some illustration of how the world travel and tourism sector might react, any lessons drawn from past experience will inevitably be imperfect.

Demand for travel - domestic or international - is driven by two fundamentals: economic factors (the incomes of travellers and the costs of the trip), and the traveller's confidence that the trip and the chosen destination are not unacceptably more risky than the alternative of staying at home. In the current circumstances, on a global scale, this latter assumption can no longer be made.

While the fear of flying may quickly abate, general security worries are now uppermost in the mind. Individuals' instincts are that the known home environment seems like the safest place to be, even if logic suggests this may not be so.

Before 11 September 2001, the global travel and tourism industry was already facing a slowdown in demand due to weak world economic trends. As an indicator of underlying macroeconomic trends, the Organisation for Economic Co-operation and Development (OECD) Composite Leading Indicators index states that historical turning points of IIP have coincided with those of entire economies.

The OECD index is expressed as an aggregated time series and smoothed to present the underlying trend. With the exception of the United Kingdom and Italy, there has been a sharp reduction in economic performance in the OECD member States in the 12 months to August 2001. This was already having a markedly negative effect on the global travel and tourism sector.

The key US economy has been on the brink of recession throughout 2001; Japan has shown no signs of emergence from economic stagnation; demand in the European Union had been flat and a downturn was in progress (except in the United Kingdom, whose economy, at least temporarily, was behaving counter-cyclically).

It is important to acknowledge that economic weakness was already causing labour demand to weaken and jobs to be lost in the travel and tourism sector, with retrenchment in the airline industry and low or no growth in tourist arrivals in some countries.

First, the immediate and sharp reduction in demand for travel had an equally immediate effect on the travel and tourism industry. Within a few weeks, well in excess of 100,000 jobs had been lost in the airline sector; hotel companies laid off staff, as did tour operators and travel agents. Knock-on effects in sectors such as catering, luxury retailers, suppliers to the aviation industry and many other subsectors partly dependent on the travelling public were evident but may take more time to work through. Such reactions were to be expected and mirror the impact of past disturbances to the travel sector.

Second, the effects of 11 September fell upon a weak global economy. They seem likely to tip many of the world's key economies into recession as a consequence. This means that demand for travel and tourism services (and thus also for labour within the sector) cannot be expected to recover in the same way as has happened in the past when such disruptions took place against the background of global economic strength.

The travel and tourism sector has thus to face a double threat - the short-term shock of sharply reduced demand ascribable to a loss of confidence, and the longer term - and potentially more profound - impact of economic recession.

Multiple travel markets

It is misleading to refer to a global travel market. There are many travel markets. Each country has its own domestic travel market, which is often by far the most important. International travel markets are similarly fragmented. Most international travel takes place to destinations within the same region as the traveller's origin (intraregional travel); travel between regions (interregional travel) forms a relatively small proportion of the total.

For example, around two-thirds of all trips abroad made by US residents are either to Mexico or Canada; 94 per cent of all German trips abroad and 83 per cent of trips abroad from the United Kingdom are to European destinations; almost 60 per cent of all Japanese trips abroad are to the Far East and South-East Asia. Long-haul travel to other regions is relatively small proportionately (although of greater proportionate worth).

Intra- and interregional travel demand has different characteristics. Thus any analyst concerned about employment in the sector in a given region or country needs to examine the components of demand for travel within and to that region/country and assess the probable impact of economic and non-economic factors on future demand levels.

Approximately four international trips in ten emanate from four countries - the United States, Germany, Japan and the United Kingdom. These four countries also account for around 40 per cent of global spending on international travel.

Since 11 September 2001 there has been no time for official statistical sources to prepare and publish any meaningful indicators relating to the travel sector. Such data as do exist derive almost solely from the travel industry - travel agents' sales, tour operators and hotel bookings, airport authorities, short-term data on passenger carryings, etc.

Even if official data did exist, the 11 September attack took place only six weeks before the ILO meeting. This is far too short a period for any meaningful trend analysis to take place which would provide a reliable guide to the future. There are no exact parallels to the terrorist attacks of September 11 and their aftermath in the history of the modern tourism industry.

In the recent past there have been wars (in Kosovo, Yugoslavia or the Gulf), terrorist incidents (Sri Lanka, Egypt or Turkey), and civil uprisings and other major disturbances (Fiji, Myanmar or China), all of which have had a considerable impact on the growth of travel and tourism. These incidents have, however, always been confined to one region of the world or one tourism destination; potential tourists have been able to change plans and redirect their travel away from the areas of unrest, and the industry - apart from within the destinations concerned - has been able to continue to draw business for and from other regions.

By contrast, the attacks in the United States represent the largest terrorist incident ever recorded. Not since the Second World War has there been a conflict situation which spans the globe in its impact and uncertainty; such a situation has never before arisen in the home of the world's most important tourism-generating market.

While the attacks took place in the United States and the offensive is currently restricted to Afghanistan, no one is sure of the arena of action, whether and to what extent it will escalate, or how long it is likely to continue..

The Gulf War, which took place in early 1991 and lasted about six weeks, is probably the closest parallel to the apparent current scale of the terrorist attacks in the United States. It also had the greatest impact on the tourism industry of any international incident in the last few decades.

International tourism, which had been growing at an average rate of 7.7 per cent in the five years prior to 1991, stalled that year and, though it did not actually decline, showed growth of only 1.2 per cent. International air travel, however, declined by some 5 per cent (and triggered a period of three years of very difficult trading conditions for the airlines).

Unsurprisingly, therewas a significant drop in travelto theMiddleEast but all other regions recorded sluggish growth, with Europe faring worst -with an increase in arrivals of only 0.1 per cent. International tourism expenditure, nevertheless, is reported to have increased by 3.7 per cent.

The brakes on tourism growth caused by the Gulf War did not in fact last long and in 1992 all regions of the world experienced growth in arrivals at similar rates to those registered in 1990, the year before the outbreak of war. Thus, in effect, the industry lost a year's expansion, before demand growth resumed.

The US tourism market is not only the world's largest in terms of tourism expenditure, but it is probably one of the most nervous in terms of its international travel behaviour. US travellers typically prefer to stay at home when there are safety concerns abroad (there were, for example, 300,000 fewer passport applications in 1991, and 400,000 fewer in 1992 than in 1990).

As a result of its size, a slowdown in US travel tends to have a significant impact on a large number of destinations. Large and established tourism countries such as the United Kingdom will obviously be affected, but so also will smaller destinations such as the islands of the Caribbean or the Pacific, where the impact may be disproportionate.

As a result of the Gulf War, travel overseas by US residents (i.e. disregarding travel to Mexico and Canada) declined in total by over 9 per cent in 1991. Among major regional destinations, Europe was the hardest hit, with a decline of nearly 22 per cent, with some countries faring particularly badly - travel to France, for example, declined by 28 per cent and to the United Kingdom by 26 per cent.

Europe was slow to recover from this fall and trips from the United States did not regain their 1990 levels until 1994. US travel to the Asia-Pacific region also fell (-3 per cent) in 1991, while travel to the Caribbean continued to grow, but nevertheless some destinations - the Bahamas, the Dominican Republic and Jamaica for example - saw huge slumps in demand.

Growth of nearly 10 per cent was registered in 1992, but this merely put total outbound numbers back to the level of two years earlier and it was not until 1993 that outbound travel exceeded the level achieved before the war. The growth of trips to Europe in 1992 was somewhat stronger than that for the market as a whole, but since the fall had been deeper, the region was still well down from 1990 levels.

The two major destinations of the United Kingdom and Germany did not again reach their 1990 numbers until 1997 and 1998, respectively. Travel to Asia held up well, however, and after stagnation in 1991 moved ahead quite strongly in the two following years.

In the early 1990s, the Japanese market had increased to over 10 million outbound travellers. It had been growing strongly prior to the Gulf War, at around 14 per cent a year for the previous two years. However, the war triggered a sharp reversal in 1991, with a decline of over 3 per cent - although it is worth noting that numbers only decreased in the first six months of the year.

Destinations furthest away from home were hit hardest, with declines to Europe being particularly sharp (minus 20 per cent in arrivals to both Germany and the United Kingdom for example). Even within Asia, numbers dropped (down by 10 per cent to Singapore, 5 per cent to Hong Kong (China) and a marginal growth to the Republic of Korea), although to the United States there was a small increase of nearly 3 percent.

The market took about a year to recover, with 1992 showing strong growth (around 11 per cent) although not reaching pre-Gulf War levels. Problems in the Japanese economy were already beginning to kick in, having their own impact on tourism demand, and by 1993 arrivals in some destinations, particularly in Europe, were only similar or marginally above numbers achieved prior to the outbreak of war.

The United Kingdom is the world's number four origin market in terms of tourism expenditure. However, in the wake of an economic slowdown in the United Kingdom at the end of the 1980s, growth in the outbound travel market had already ground almost to a halt before the beginning of the hostilities in the Gulf and economic conditions continued to exert a brake on travel behaviour in 1990 and 1991.

At the same time, travellers from the United Kingdom tend to be among the more resilient in the face of uncertainties overseas, and the impact on travel of the Gulf War was generally not that great. There was an overall small decline (1 per cent) with, unsurprisingly, long-haul travel the worst affected. But travel to the United States grew, albeit slowly, as did some of the major leisure destinations within Europe.

By 1992, however, growth resumed quite strongly, with the long-haul destinations showing the strongest performance. The events that took place in Tiananmen Square in Beijing in June 1989 drew the world's attention and demolished a tourism industry in China that had been growing reasonably strongly, if somewhat erratically, during the second half of the decade.

Leisure travel to China was most seriously affected, leading to many cancellations. Foreign arrivals declined by over a fifth from 1988 and among China's major markets, only Taiwan (China) held up. Concern at the events was particularly strong in North America and the West, as well as in Japan, and the reaction from these markets was immediate - down 40 per cent from Japan, and a reduction in the high 20 per cent range from the United States, United Kingdom and Germany.

Martial law was lifted at the beginning of 1990 but China's image continued to deter many visitors. Memories are short, however, and with an uneventful anniversary of the Tiananmen, visitors began to return and by the end of the year the overall arrivals count showed a healthy 20 per cent increase.

The major Western markets were somewhat slower to return and although they were all back to modest growth, it was all at single-digit levels. Only Japan, which had shown the sharpest fall in 1989, showed an instant recovery. Nevertheless, in 1991 - when travel around the world was tempered by the Gulf crisis -the full bounce-back came, with Germany (up by 65 per cent), the United Kingdom (up by 45 per cent), Japan (38 per cent) and the United States.

In November 1997 the tourism industry was targeted directly when terrorists killed 58 tourists at the temple of Queen Hatshepsut at Luxor in Egypt. Among the tourists were a large number of Swiss visitors. This, together with incidents in Turkey in the latter half of the 1990s, represents one of only a few occasions when tourists themselves have been the specific target of terrorist atrocities rather than being inadvertently caught up in the wider act of terrorism.

Before the terrorist incident at Luxor, Egypt had been experiencing strong growth in its tourism arrivals, with an increase of over 20 per cent a year since 1994. Because the attack occurred towards the end of the year, marginal growth was recorded even in 1997. However, the incident had an immediate impact in instantly shutting down the flow of tourists to Egypt, travel advisories were issued and the industry came to a virtual standstill.

The effects lingered through the whole of the next year and 1998 saw a decline in arrivals of almost 13 per cent. Almost all markets (with the exception of Arab countries) were badly affected. Japan showed the worst decline (75 per cent), but business from Europe was also badly affected, possibly because the attack had mainly hit Europeans; there was, for example, a decline of 38 per cent from Egypt's major European market, Germany, and 28 per cent from the United Kingdom. Visitors from the United States declined by 13 per cent.

Once again, within a year the tourism industry had bounced back and 1999 saw overall growth of 30 per cent. Japan and Germany were particularly strong with rises of over 100 per cent, but all traditional tourism markets, including other European markets and the United States, did well.

Egypt's international tourism receipts followed a broadly similar pattern to arrivals. They produced a stronger result in 1997, but the decline in 1998 was sharper. Equally, the bounce-back in 1999 was better than that for arrivals. However, with no growth in 1997 and a decline in 1998, Egypt had in effect lost two years' tourism growth in the wake of the terrorism in Luxor.

Although confidence had returned by 1999 and arrivals reached record numbers, growth that year, although good, was insufficient to bring tourism back to the levels it would have reached had the massacre not occurred.

World's tourism markets provide no hard and fast rules on what can be expected from the current crisis, some generalizations can nevertheless be made:

- the impact on tourism of a terrorist incident is instantaneous;
- nonetheless, it is difficult to halt international tourism growth;

— the tourism world is sufficiently large and diverse that even in the face of a major incident, travel can continue to grow;

— after the conclusion of an incident, travel markets can pick up relatively quickly;

— the immediate impact tends to last for between one and two years;

— while growth recovers, there is a lag effect and projected business volumes are only attained later than originally expected;

— when problems occur in one particular destination, tourists tend to redirect to a different destination;

— in times of crisis, long-haul travel suffers more than short-haul;

— since the largest share of international travel is intraregional, a large proportion of such travel may be relatively unaffected;

— because they dominate international tourism, the behaviour of a few tourism markets particularly the United States, Germany, Japan and the United Kingdom - have a major impact on the performance of most tourism destinations, large or small, established or embryonic;

— the characteristics of these markets vary; in general terms the European market tends to be less nervous in the face of international terrorism than either the United States or Japan.

In order to illustrate the immediate and potential longer term effects of the current crisis on international travel and on travel industries, the following are some brief examples of current trends in the travel sectors of the four leading origin markets of the United States, Germany, Japan and the United Kingdom. Although only illustrative, these experiences may be taken to reflect trends in other countries in the same region. For obvious reasons, the immediate impact on the US travel and tourism industry has been dramatic.

The Japanese travel market is the most important in Asia; it has also been resilient to pervasive economic weaknesses in Japan itself. While there is no evidence that Japan is likely to emerge from the economic doldrums in the near future, annual Japanese outbound travel trip volumes had been holding up well, reaching almost 18 million in 2000.

Reactions by the Japanese travel market include:

— In the two weeks following 11 September, 290,000 people cancelled planned overseas trips - approximately 20 per cent of the mean monthly outbound total.

— Trans-Pacific travel, both to the US mainland and to Hawaii, fell sharply. To the mainland there were falls of 20-25 per cent in the month after the attack; to Hawaii the decline in the four-week period was 50 per cent.

— To other destinations, the reaction has been less severe; airlines in Japan have reported that they expect demand for air travel to other international destinations to fall by 5 per cent by the end of the year, while domestic travel, which had been strong anyway during 2001, is predicted to gain from the crisis.

— While details remain sketchy, the indications are that the main initial fear of the Japanese international travellers was of flying; the aftermath of 11 September, and in particular the military action in Afghanistan, is converting that into a more general concern about security abroad, and the predictions are that demand for international trips will remain depressed in Japan until the early months of 2002 at least.

Japan's travel market seems set to be affected over the medium term. Demand for trans-Pacific travel will be most affected; past history suggests that travel to Europe will also fall, while demand for travel within the North-East/South-East Asian region is likely to fare better, at least once the winter is past and the more popular months for travelling arrive - probably starting with the second quarter of 2002.

In terms of the number of foreign trips made, Germany is by far the world's largest travel market. However, 94 per cent of German trips abroad are within Europe. Interregional travel by Germans, though large in absolute numbers, is relatively quite modest in comparison with intraregional business. Since 11 September, the reactions of the German travel market have included the following:

— In the immediate aftermath of 11 September a wave of cancellations hit the German travel trade.

— The worst-affected destinations were the United States, the eastern Mediterranean and the Middle East, and North Africa.

— Reports within ten days of the attack indicated that around 25 per cent of planned trips to the United States had been cancelled and that there had also been initial cancellations to Turkey, Egypt, Dubai and Tunisia.

— However, within three weeks of the 11 September attack, the German international travel market was reporting the first signs of recovery, except for the United States and Middle East.

— Looking to 2002, there is a feeling that general German travel demand will return to more normal levels. There may well be a switch in demand away from eastern Mediterranean destinations towards Spain, but even to the United States it is now expected that demand will return to normal by the middle of 2002.

In short, it appears that German travellers are likely to get over their initial fears about the safety of travel quite quickly. There has to date been no material threat to Germany and provided that remains the case, the mature German travel market seems likely to see no more than a short-term decline in demand before normal levels of activity return.

The United Kingdom is the world's fourth largest market for international travel. In long-haul travel, however, it is especially important - the largest in Europe for travel to the.Asia-Pacific region, for example, and the second largest overseas market to the United States after Japan. Initial reactions to 11 September by the UK travel market have included the following:

— As with Germany there was an immediate wave of travel cancellations and postponements; in the last week of September new bookings for winter travel were 33 per cent below those of a year previously; for summer 2002, advance bookings were 45 per cent down.

— Some specialist operators reported that bookings for Middle Eastern destinations were 50 per cent down in the first two weeks, and cancellations were running at 25 per cent.

— BAA plc, the owner of London's main airports, reported a 26 per cent fall in transatlantic traffic for the month of September and of just under 7 per cent for other long-haul destinations.

— However, there are also indications that the UK market is showing signs of recovery along the same lines as in Germany - for destinations which are not seen as notably risky; winter skiing holidays to European destinations, for example, are reported to be selling well again in mid-October; travel agents, having reported a 30 per cent drop in business during September, reported that business had started to recover.

Few destinations have yet been able to know how to react, since hard market information is scarce at so early a stage. In principle, however, the reaction of tourism destination countries has reflected their visitor profile. Beyond the initial reality of weak demand worldwide, the most exposed destinations are those for which the United States is a prime or the primary origin market.

This means that countries such as Canada, Mexico, much of the Caribbean, key European countries such as the United Kingdom, and some destinations in Asia and the Pacific are likely to suffer worst. Secondly, destinations which draw their visitors from long-haul origin markets (e.g. Australia) are also likely to see especially weak markets.

Immediately after 11 September, the Australian Tourist Commission (ATC) withdrew its tactical advertising campaigns in the United States, Europe, Asia and Japan as global tourism demand slumped. The ATC will monitor individual market reactions closely. It expects that Australia may benefit from some destination switching, e.g. UK travellers going to Australia instead of to the United States; it also expects travel from the United States to be very weak, but believes that Asian origins such as Japan should not be badly affected for long.

The Tourism Authority of Thailand (TAT) immediately adjusted its marketing plans after 11 September. Visitors from the United States and Middle East are expected to fall sharply and the marketing emphasis will shift to origin markets closer to home, such as the Association of South-East Asian Nations (ASEAN) member countries, East Asia and Oceania.

The former marketing budget for the United States will be switched to these markets and campaigns will target groups such as those who were intending to go to the United States, young travellers, honeymooners, long-stay senior travellers and also the corporate meetings market. These two brief cases illustrate two general reactions:

(a) marketing funds will be switched from unpromising origin markets to more promising ones, and

(b) pragmatic and opportunistic adjustments will be made to marketing campaigns; destinations will seek to exploit comparative advantages and distance themselves from as many of the current geographical, religious and cultural risks as possible. Tourism destination marketing has always been competitive; it is likely to be ruthlessly so in the next few months.

The travel industry

There is no room here to list all the effects on the industry worldwide, but the following examples serve as useful indicators:

— Marriott Hotels in the United States claims that revenues for September are 25 per cent below those of the previous year (but, importantly, also states that they were 10 per cent down on 2000 prior to 11 September, reflecting a weakening national economy).

— Marriott also claims that, of the 2 million employees in the United States' hotel sector, 50 per cent have either lost their jobs or have been put on short-term/part-time work.

— If demand for travel within the United States remains 35 per cent below normal, as it has in the month following 11 September, Carlson Companies claims that 3.8 million jobs would be lost in the country; if the situation "improves" to a point where the demand is only 20 per cent below last year, job losses would total 2.2 million (around 12 per cent of the total sectoral employment of 19 million).

— The American Society of Travel Agents (ASTA) has predicted that travel agents' revenues for 2001 will be $9.9 billion compared with $13.4 billion in 2000; for 2002 ASTA is predicting revenues of just $5 billion and potential job losses in excess of 100,000.

— The Air Transport Association of the United States expects that total revenue passenger miles will be down by 39 per cent in the fourth quarter of this year, down 23 per cent in the first quarter of 2002 and down 13 per cent in the second quarter; by the third quarter traffic will be back at 2001 levels.

— In addition to the US tourism industry, there will be substantial job losses across some European countries as travel agents and tour operators shed labour. There may be some similar effects in Asian markets such as Japan.

— Club Méditerranée has announced the winter closure of 15 of its villages in the Caribbean, Central America, Africa, Middle East, Europe and one in Malaysia, and a 50 per cent cut in its planned capital expenditure programme next year, in the face of reduced bookings, plus the closure of four to five more where there are prospects of substantial losses arising. This will result in a 15 per cent reduction of worldwide capacity.

— Nonetheless, there are also more positive signs. Leading members of the German tour operating and travel agency business by the second week of October were reporting a return of travel demand to European destinations and to some long-haul destinations (mention was made of strong demand for travel to the Canary Islands, Austria, Italy, France, Switzerland and, in the long-haul segment, to Kenya, South Africa and the Caribbean); they point out that German travel to the United States represents a small proportion of their revenue and thus exhibit few public fears about the financial effects of weak demand for the United States on their businesses.

— On a global basis, however, the effects of economic recession on travel should also be borne in mind; while 11 September made matters worse, demand was already weakening in many markets and some job losses would have happened anyway.

— The airline industry (the subject of another ILO meeting) is likely to lose more money in 2001 than it has ever done in one year, sustain further losses in 2002, see capacity cut on the North Atlantic by perhaps 20 per cent and be put into a position from which it will find it hard to "prime the pump" of returning demand in due course.

— There will be some upward pressure on air fares due to poorer aircraft utilization and higher security and insurance costs, but their effects could be less than feared if fuel prices remain low.

— While the greatest pressure currently is on the airline industry, sectors such as hotels, restaurants, car rental and cruise ships are also at risk, as are travel trade members in tour operating and travel agencies; such subsectors derive their demand from underlying travel volumes and all are at risk.

Furthermore, the loss of US customers and (in some markets) possibly Japanese customers also will have wider impacts in areas such as specialist retailing ("designer" and luxury products, or cultural centres such as London's theatreland, for example, which rely on travellers for many of their sales).

In Asia, an immediate fall in demand also took place but, again, there are some indications of recovery in regional markets; once again, long-haul travel, and especially trans-Pacific travel, remains the weakest element. Tourism destinations across the world are adjusting their marketing programmes to address origin markets nearby; marketing to long-haul origins (with some exceptions) is likely to be reduced for the next few months.

The travel and tourism sector has undergone a sharp reduction in employment as a direct consequence of 11 September but this should be seen against the background of weak global economies. The knock-on effects for secondary employment in related sectors may also be quite severe.

In the United States, job losses may quickly reach 10 per cent of sectoral employment and could go further in the months to come. In Europe and Asia the effects are likely to be less severe; in some destination regions which are dependent upon the US travel market, severe employment losses are to be expected.

Travel to the United States is, for the immediate future, going to be severely curtailed from almost all markets. A vision of the collapse of the twin towers of the World Trade Center has imprinted itself on the minds of the world's travellers; together with the threat of chemical or biological attacks and the real fear of anthrax, the US industry is very vulnerable; an immediate recovery seems unlikely.

In Europe, the world's biggest tourism destination, travel is already showing some signs of recovery. For the dominant intraregional travel, under the best-case scenario it seems likely that travel will not be badly dented. Europeans will continue to travel within their own continent. While travel to the eastern Mediterranean and the whole of the Middle East is unlikely to come back in the short term, destinations such as Spain, France, Italy and Portugal may well benefit from substitution destination choice.

The US market is, however, a significant element of Europe's tourism, particularly in key cities such as London and Paris and tourist destinations such as Venice and Stratford-on-Avon. It will clearly be some time before travel from this market begins to pick up. These travellers are recognized as high spenders, and a reduction in their number could have a considerable impact on the up-market hotel groups as well as a knock-on effect for a large number of industry segments such as taxi drivers, the retail trade and the entertainment industry.

Equally, long-haul travel from Asia, especially from Japan - whose spending patterns also have a big impact at the top end of the tourism industry - can be expected to be lacklustre for the next six months at least. Such events would both choke demand from Asia and North America, and completely change the intraregional travel patterns of Europeans themselves. Depending on the scale and location of any violations, travel within Europe would, at the very least, be redirected away from the scene of action and domestic travel would probably benefit.

Business travel - a major element of intra-European travel and from North America and Japan - would equally feel the brunt. Companies which have already curbed employees' travel in response to the current economic climate would be likely to impose further restrictions -again having a major impact on the top end of the industry.

The Middle East's tourism industry is perhaps in the least enviable position of all regions at the current time. Until recently, countries such as Egypt, Lebanon and Dubai were growing strongly but the 11 September events have pushed the entire region into the spotlight. The prospects for tourism for the present look poor.

Intraregional travel could be relatively unaffected but the leisure markets from the West and Japan are unlikely to show any interest in visiting the region until the current crisis stabilizes.

Tourism to Africa will inevitably suffer as a result of the current crisis, particularly because most high-revenue tourism to the continent is long-haul. It is this long-haul market that is likely to take most time to recover from the current crisis. The major market for sub-Saharan Africa is Europe, particularly the United Kingdom; providing the global economic downturn is not too sharp, there could well be some substitution to Africa away from other areas such as the Middle East or India, that could be regarded as more "risky".

Tourism in the Asia-Pacific region is primarily intraregional and, in the best-case scenario, this is likely to pick up fairly quickly. This market is led by Japan, however, and much will depend on that country's reaction. The Japanese market has so far been relatively immune to the country's economic troubles and, barring further terrorist outrages, past precedent suggests that Japanese travel will resume; the region should benefit from a desire to travel near to home.

For many countries in Asia the European market, particularly the United Kingdom, is of major importance. While there has been nervousness within Europe for all long-haul travel, barring further incidents, travel should begin to resume to areas that are not seen as fundamentally risky. To a certain extent this is related to how close the destination is to the scene of action in Afghanistan.

Countries in Asia which traditionally receive large numbers of tourists from the United States - the Philippines, Japan and many of the Pacific islands - will need to direct their marketing efforts elsewhere since for the foreseeable future it is unlikely that the US market will venture as far as Asia.

The Caribbean is heavily dependent on the US market (which accounts for around half of total arrivals in the region and a larger proportion of visitor expenditure) and for the short term at least it will suffer from the fact that Americans simply are not travelling. Europe, accounting for 24 per cent of arrivals, is very important for some destinations.

Countries which have a high proportion ofEuropeans in theirvisitor mix -Grenada,Barbadosand Saint Lucia, for example - will do better and are currently targeting the European market with bargain offers which should increase demand.

The World Travel and Tourism Council (WTTC) estimates that there are some 207 million people employed worldwide in the travel and tourism economy, equivalent to just over 8 per cent of global employment. A 10 per cent reduction in the volume of business - WTTC's "best guess" as to the impact of the 11 September attack - would result in an estimated 8.8 million job losses, of which 1.1 million would be in the United States and 1.2 million in the European Union.

Over the last thirty years, international tourism, has grown more rapidly than any other service sector and, in terms of receipts, is now the second most important service sector (after banking) in world trade. At the same time, it is the most labour intensive of the service sectors and provides employment to a very substantial part of the working population of a great number of countries, both inside and outside the OECD.

This expansion has taken place under conditions, by and large, remarkably free from protectionist measures and distortions of competition, at least in OECD Member countries, and this relative lack of barriers has made a substantial contribution to the speed at which the sector has evolved. By comparison with other service sectors, tourism has remained virtually free from the burden of 'sacred cows' designed to preserve special privileges, and where measures perceived as obstacles to the liberalisation of the sector are observed, their rationale is very frequently unconnected with tourism itself, having been introduced for quite other purposes.

Nevertheless, it is important that, if the growth of international tourism is to be sustained, this situation of relative liberalisation which prevails within the OECD area should be maintained and, where possible, extended beyond the limits of the OECD. It is also desirable that the same freedom should be encouraged in the tourism-related industries, without which tourism itself would be impossible, most notably in the realm of passenger transport.

To help in the preservation of this situation, it appears important that there should be as much transparency as possible on those restrictive or discriminatory measures that do exist, so that new measures should not creep in and that existing measures and relevant developments may be kept under review so that those which distort or eliminate competition or which unnecessarily impede the traveller can be progressively phased out.

The Tourism Committee of the OECD has, since its inception, been principally concerned with the liberalisation of international tourism within the OECD area, and with the facilitation of travel between Member countries. At the beginning of the eighties, however, there was a renewed impetus in the Organisation as a whole in the direction of liberalisation in trade in services.

The Trade Committee initiated a general work programme concerning existing obstacles to liberalising the various service sectors and the development of a set of general concepts which could serve as a framework for the evaluation of the service industries as a whole, initially within the OECD and then, after the Punta del Este meeting in September 1986, in the wider context of work on services in GATT.

At much the same time, the Committee on Capital Movements and Invisible Transactions (CMIT) which is responsible for the Codes of Liberalisation of Current Invisible Operations (CLIO) and of Capital Movements (CLCM) [which, with the National Treatment Instrument, currently being strengthened by the Committee on International Investment and Multinational Enterprises (CIME), form the basis for all liberalisation objectives within the OECD], started work on updating them and making them more responsive to present day conditions.

These initiatives were vigorously endorsed by OECD Ministers at recent annual meetings of the Council at ministerial level. Being responsible for one of the major service sectors, the Tourism Committee considered it a matter of high priority to participate in this work and elaborated in 1982 and 1983 the first version of an Inventory of Obstacles to International Tourism in the OECD Area.

In 1984, a joint CMIT/Tourism Committee Working Group was established to examine matters concerning the liberalisation of international tourism, with specific reference to the updating of the relevant sections of CLIO. The outcome was an extensive enlargement of the obligations of Member countries under the "Travel and Tourism" Item of CLIO which were adopted by the Council in September 1985.

Leading on from the work on the Inventory and CLIO, the Tourism Committee developed during 1984 and 1985 an Instrument for international tourism policy; this Instrument, the OECD Decision-Recommendation on International Tourism Policy was adopted by the Council in November 1985. This Instrument sets a number of objectives to be reached through continuous monitoring of the situation as well as periodic reviews of measures and reports on progress towards its implementation, ending in an overall review and updating of the Instrument itself.

The 1984 Inventory was a first try at something which had not previously been attempted. As a result, it was not envisaged to be exhaustive, its arrangement was entirely pragmatic, and it was not easy for an outsider to use. The purposes of the Inventory, while similar to those of the original 1984 version, have been widened, as a result both of experience and of changes in the work programme of the Committee.

It is still first and foremost a catalogue of measures which do not appear to be entirely in line with the basic principles of liberalisation of international tourism as set out in the various OECD Instruments mentioned above. As such, it forms a compendium for anyone, inside or outside the Organisation, who needs to know what the positions are in Member countries, with regard to both the individual traveller and the tourism or tourism-related enterprise. It thus serves the prime purpose of providing transparency. However, it has a number of other purposes. These include:

a) Background information for the preparation of the Committee's report to the Council of the OECD on the overall situation prevailing in the OECD area ;

b) Assistance in the development and evolution of the OECD Instruments mentioned earlier, which are directed towards increasing liberalisation of the service sectors;

c) The provision of a base for the revision and extension of the Decision-Recommendation of the Council on International Tourism Policy ;

d) Support to the negotiators from Member countries in the Uruguay Round in their work towards developing a General Agreement on Trade in Services (GATS) for which the framework agreement is scheduled to be completed by the end of 1990.

The first section of the Inventory, dealing with measures affecting international travellers, is particularly associated with the Travel and Tourism Item of CLIO which takes up all matters associated with means of payment and currency allowances. The second section, which is mainly concerned with restrictions and discrimination relating to non-national enterprises wishing to offer their services to customers in other OECD countries, is more closely related to the CLCM and the National Treatment Instrument (although the importation of tourist publicity material comes under CLIO).

For this reason, any measure recorded in the lists of exceptions to national treatment, or associated with a reservation on inward direct investment, but which has a particularly severe impact on tourism, is so annotated in the Inventory. It is important to note that references to "national treatment" in the Inventory follow the OECD definition, i.e. they relate to discrimination against enterprises already operating in an OECD country.

It will be noted that each major item in the Inventory has an annotation in the "Remarks" column, giving the "category" of impediment associated with the measures under the item. This is, inter alia, to facilitate the use of the Inventory for assisting the work towards GATS. These are specifically related to the OECD publication Elements of a Conceptual Framework for Trade in Services which covers, inter alia, market access, transparency, national treatment, non-discrimination, service monopolies, and trade-distorting measures or practices.

However, they also take account of the overall text on "Negotiations on Trade in Services" agreed in Montreal at the end of 1988 and in Geneva in 1989, which forms the agreed base for work towards GATS. The Montreal text highlights the principles of transparency, national treatment, most favoured nation (MFN), non-discrimination, and market access, and also contains sections on progressive liberalisation, the increasing participation of developing countries, safeguards and exceptions, and regulatory situations.

While the principles of non-discrimination and MFN treatment are not specifically referred to in the Inventory, they are among its basic underlying elements, i.e. there should, if possible, be no distinction between national and non-national persons or enterprises, but there should in any case be no distinction among those of other OECD countries.

At the present stage, the Inventory does not take up issues relating to non-Member countries; hence discrimination either against or in favour of such countries or groups of countries is not a concern of the Inventory. It should also be noted that in the GATS context "national treatment" is not limited to enterprises which are already established, but, to quote the text verbatim, "national treatment means that the services exports and/or exporters of any signatory are accorded in the market of any other signatory, in respect of all laws, regulations and administrative practices, treatment 'no less favourable' than that accorded domestic services or services providers in the same market".

The present Inventory consists of measures introduced through legislation, regulations or administrative practices by the governments of Member countries or, in cases of countries with a federal structure, by the territorial sub-divisions within them. It does not include:

a) Measures introduced by local government entities;

b) Measures introduced by private or semi-governmental organisations;

c) Measures introduced by the governments or organisations of non-OECD countries; and

d) Measures which are solely concerned with persons or enterprises from non-OECD countries.

At various times it has been discussed whether any of the foregoing should be included in the Inventory and the Committee is currently engaged in examining comparable measures of discrimination in non-OECD countries but it has been decided that it would be undesirable to delay the completion of the present Inventory to accommodate this work, which is only at an early stage.

The Inventory does not include any measure which:

a) Only relates to enterprises or nationals of non-Member countries (e.g. visa requirements in certain countries);

b) Relates to the general operation of national immigration and employment policies in which tourism and/or tourism-related industries do not have a status different from any other sector of the economy, except insofar as they relate to the entry of individual travellers or to the temporary entry of persons engaged in providing tourism services;

c) Relates to the overall structure of international aviation;

d) Derives from national policies concerning inward direct investment under which tourism and/or tourism-related industries are not granted a status different from any other sector of the economy, unless their impact is particularly severe upon tourism.

The Tourism Committee recognises that the organisation of bilateral services, route allocation and route structures, the operation of foreign-controlled airlines within countries and other matters relating to the international structure of civil aviation do not fall within its competence. However, it considers that these matters can act as an impediment to the growth of international tourism, and that steps should be taken by the appropriate bodies to remedy any possible effects of this nature. The Inventory should include:

— Matters where the abuse of a dominant position of an airline introduces distortion in other sectors of the industry by, for example, its control of travel agencies, hotel chains and reservation systems;

— Matters where facilities at airports are provided to foreign airlines in a way that discriminates against them;

— Matters where the national carrier has preferential tax/subsidies status or benefits from preferences to transport government personnel."

In the cases of inward direct investment, and of immigration and employment policies, the exclusion was to avoid duplication of work with other bodies within the OECD, where the measures recorded or examined were of a general or trans-sectoral nature. This applies particularly to work undertaken by the CIME, the CMIT, the Manpower and Social Affairs Committee and the Working Party on Migration.

However, where tourism and tourism-related industries are treated in a less favourable manner than other industries, where they are particularly seriously affected or where they are hit by measures introduced for reasons unrelated to tourism (as in the case of visa requirements), the measures are included in the Inventory.

An "obstacle" for the purpose of this Inventory is defined as a measure derived from legislation, regulations or administrative practices which:

a) Restricts or impedes the individual traveller from travelling abroad as a user of tourist services, or

b) Introduces discriminatory treatment intended to encourage the residents of a country to travel in their own country rather than abroad, or to visit particular countries rather than others; or

c) By requiring conditions less favourable than those accorded to the national enterprises of the host country, prevents or impedes an enterprise established in a Member country:

- From selling/providing tourist services in another Member country; or
- From establishing itself through new enterprises or through acquisition of existing enterprises (e.g. authorisations, licences, etc.); or
- Once established in the host country, from selling/provided services.

d) By requiring conditions less favourable than those accorded to the nationals of the host country, prevents or impedes a professional national of another Member country operating on his own account from selling/providing tourist services in the host country. It then sets out three types of impediments to enterprises wishing to offer tourism services to the customer:

- firstly, by preventing them from entering the market place at all;
- secondly, by placing restrictions on the type of organisation they may use to market their services; and
- thirdly, by putting enterprises owned by nationals at an advantage over similar enterprises which are not so owned.

— finally, it deals with impediments to individuals offering their own services in other OECD countries.

International tourism in the OECD area is, by comparison with other service sectors, remarkably free from protectionist and discriminatory practices. Nevertheless, it is incumbent upon all who are engaged in this sector to remain vigilant against the creeping growth of measures, often introduced for purposes wholly unconnected with tourism, which work against the.o open and competitive structure which exists at present. If the existence of a list of measures which are currently acting as impediments can assist in this process, its production will have been fully justified.

The OECD Codes of Liberalisation have the legal status of OECD Decisions which are binding on all the Members. Accordingly, OECD Members are expected to take whatever steps are necessary to ensure that the obligations accepted are honoured. The strength of the Codes lies also in the determination of the Member countries to pursue the objectives of the Codes and to make active use of them as instruments for international economic co-oepration.

The Codes provide a framework of notification, examination and consultation through which observance of their prescriptions can be effectively monitored and achieved. They also serve as a yardstick against which liberalisation progress can be judged. Although the two Codes differ from each other in certain respects, the general principles that govern these two instruments are broadly the same.

In adhering to the Codes, Member countries undertake to remove restrictions on specified lists of current invisible operations and capital movements. The ultimate objective is that residents of different Member countries should be as free to transact business with each other as are residents of the same country. This objective, however, is not immediate nor unqualified. Neither could the Codes' approach to liberalisation be described as doctrinaire.

Rather, it seeks to engage Member countries in a process of progressive liberalisation, allowing reasonable scope for countries in different circumstances to move towards the ultimate objective in different ways and at varying speeds, taking account of the specific economic circumstances they face.

"Liberalisation" in the sense of the Codes means the abolition of governmental restrictions on the conclusion or execution of both transactions and transfers with respect to the operations specified in the Codes. In other words, the obligation to liberalise goes beyond the requirement that the transfer of funds to and from abroad should be free from exchange control restrictions. It also requires that the underlying transactions themselves should not be frustrated by legal or administrative regulations.

Nonetheless, restrictions may be imposed if they are judged necessary to meet certain concerns, such as the maintenance of public order or the protection of essential security interests (Article 3). The Codes also permit Member countries to verify the authenticity of transactions and transfers, as a means of preventing evasion of their laws or regulations (Article 5). This is a most important point and one that is not always fully understood.

The Codes do not interfere with the freedom of Member countries to prevent illegal activities such as fraud, money-laundering, or evasion of taxation laws, and verification procedures may be maintained for any of these purposes as well as for gathering statistics. Of course, any such verification should be carried out in a non-discriminatory manner and simplified as far as possible so as not to frustrate legitimate operations.

The liberalisation obligations apply only to operations between the residents of two OECD Member countries adhering to the Codes. The obligations do not apply to operations between non-residents, nor between residents of the same country even if one party to the operation is the affiliate of a company owned or controlled by non-residents.

Non-residents are to be dealt with on an equal footing with their resident counterparts but Members are not required to extend better treatment to non-residents than to their own residents. There is no duty to extend liberalisation beyond the Members of the OECD, although adherents to the Code should endeavour to do so for member countries of the International Monetary Fund (Article 1d).

Finally, in adhering to the Codes, Members commit themselves, in principle, to ensuring that the Code obligations are fulfilled at all levels of government within their country. As countries with a federal constitution, however, both, the United States and Canada felt the need for special arrangements to cover this aspect of their situation. These special arrangements recognise the constitutional limits to the power of the federal government in those countries to dispose of matters within the purview of the Codes.

Although nowhere is it explicitly stated as such in either Code, the principle of "national treatment" can be safely said to lie at the heart of the Code approach to liberalisation. The national treatment principle requires that, in like circumstances, the authorities of Member countries shall adopt and apply laws, regulations and policies that treat non-residents no less favourably than residents.

The ultimate objective of the Codes is to enable residents of different OECD countries to deal as readily with each other as residents of the same country in all the operations covered. The national treatment principle finds expression notably in regard to inward direct investment and establishment. From the viewpoint of liberalising international trade in services, the freedom for international direct investment and establishment occupies a place of special importance.

While some services can be readily provided across national boundaries, many require the establishment of an operating presence in the country where the services are to be sold. In the banking and financial services sector, an established.o presence may be necessary if foreign firms are to be able to achieve effective access to a given market, to offer a full range of services and to compete with national institutions on an equal footing.

The Codes distinguish between "liberalisation" and "deregulation" in the sense that the obligation to liberalise does not entail an obligation to give up national regulation, nor to harmonise on an international standard. By the same token, the lack of internationally-agreed standards of regulation however regrettable-is not recognised as a reason for delaying.o liberalisation which is intended to create opportunities for cross-border operations.

Thus a degree of mutual recognition of regulatory standards might be said to be implicit in the Code approach, although considerable scope is allowed for national regulation, especially if operated on a basis that does not discriminate against non-residents.

An important feature of the Codes is that liberalisation measures-as well as restrictions-are to be applied to all Member countries on a non-discriminatory basis (Articles 8 and 9). As noted in a report by the drafters of the Codes, "there should be no attempt by countries to bargain with their neighbours individually in securing reciprocal concessions on specific items. Reciprocity is to be sought only over the whoxle geographical area and over the wide range of visible and invisible transactions-nothing less.

Even Members which are in economic difficulties and cannot themselves liberalise must not be discriminated against and must continue to receive the economic advantages of liberalisation granted by other Members. In recent years, reciprocity has come to be used by some Members to support the efforts of their national enterprises to establish themselves in foreign markets.

Reciprocity of this kind has been most prevalent in the banking and financial services sector, where particular problems arise from the existence of different institutional structures in Member countries and where some Members have taken the view that reciprocity requirements may contribute to increasing the overall degree of liberalisation.

The Organisation dealt with this issue by adopting a decision in July 1986 under which reciprocity measures and practices are considered to have a somewhat different status from that of restrictions against which reservations can be lodged, but the procedures to be applied to them are essentially the same. Accordingly, the measures and practices of reciprocity existing as of the date of the Council Decision are recorded in a special annex to the Code and regularly examined by the Organisation with a view to their eventual elimination.

Bibliography

American Society of Travel Agents, *ASTA Travel Agent Manual,* Alexandria, VA: ASTA, 1995.

Andereck, Kathleen L., "The Impacts of Tourism on Natural Resources", *Parks and Recreation, 28* (6), 26-32, 1993.

Ap, John & Crompton, John L., "Developing and Testing a Tourism Impact Scale", *Journal of Travel Research* November, *37* (2), 120-130, 1998.

Bush, Melinda, "Panel Analyzes Trends in the Evolving Agent-Hotelier Relationship, *Travel Weekly, 48* (47), 25-30, 1989.

Carey, Sandra & Gountas, Y., "Tour Operators and Destination Sustainability", *Tourism Management, 18* (7), 425-431, 1997.

Chmura, Gail L., & Ross, Neil W., *The Environmental Impacts of Marinas and Their Boats,* National Oceanic and Atmospheric Administration Office of Sea Grant, U.S. Dept. of Commerce; University of Rhode Island, 1978.

Deady, Tim & Schwartzman, M. T., "Ecotourism: Traveling to Save the Planet", *Travel Weekly, 49* (34), 105-108, 1990.

Del Rosso, Laura, "Responsible Tourism is Focus of Travel Expo: 1997 New Travel Expo", *Travel Weekly 56* (14), 10-13, 1997.

Gee, Chuck Y., Makens, James C. Makens, & Choy, Dexter J.L., *The Travel Industry,* New York: Van Nostrand Reinhold, 1989.

Goeldner, Charles R., "The 1998 Travel Outlook", *Journal of Travel Research, 36* (2), 58-62, 1997.

Johnson, Scott C., "Travel Services; Industry Overview", *U.S. Department of Commerce, U.S. Industrial Outlook,* 41-52, 1994.

Lassiter, Eric, "Spotlighting Agency Networks: Definition Developed by Standardized Travel Agency Reporting Group", *Travel Weekly, 55* (51), S7-S8, 1996, June 27.

Lewis, Ira, Semeijn, Janjaap, & Talalayevsky, Alexander, "The Impact of Technology on Travel Agents", *American Society of Transportation and Logistics Transportation Journal, 37* (4), 20-29, 1998, June 12.

Noack, David R., "Planes, Trains, and Cruise Lines: The Net has Become a Cornucopia of Travel Information and Services", *Internet World, 7* (7), 82-86, 1996.

Schulz, Christopher, "Hotels and Travel Agents: The New Partnership", *The Cornell Hotel and Restaurant Administration Quarterly, 35* (2), 45-50, 1994.

Index

American Society of Travel Agents (ASTA), 275
Association of Southeast Asian Nations (ASEAN), 135
Australian and New Zealand Standard Industrial Classification (ANZSIC), 2
Australian Antarctic Science (AAS), 143
Australian Tourist Commission (ATC), 273

Capital Movements and Invisible Transactions (CMIT), 283
Codes of Liberalisation of Current Invisible Operations (CLIO), 283
Colonialism, dynamics of, 128
Commercial Antarctic tourism, 141
Committee on International Investment and Multinational Enterprises (CIME), 283
Corporate Social Responsibility (CSR), 20
Cost-cutting programme, 235

Department of Tourism (DoT), 242
Domestic Tourism Expenditure Survey (DTES), 240
Domestic tourism, 7

Electronic technology, 128

Financial education programmes, 32

General Agreement on Trade in Services (GATS), 127
Global tourism, 28
Global travel market, 261
Gross Domestic Product (GDP), 6

Inbound tourism, 238
Income, dynamic sources of, 127
International Association of Antarctica Tour Operators (IAATO), 142
International tourism, 263
International Visitor Survey (IVS), 237
Intra-regional tourism, 225

Laden, Osama Bin, 258
Local conservation programmes, 28

Martial lawm 266
Mass tourism, 128
Modern international tourism, 128
Modernization, 234
Most Favoured Nation (MFN), 286

On-line intranet system, 31
Opportunistic adjustments, 274
Organisation for Economic Cooperation and Development (OECD), 3
Real domestic tourism, 241

Scandinavian Airlines (SAS), 15
Severe Acute Respiratory Syndrome (SARS), 221
Sex tourism, 135
Singapore Tourism Board's (STB), 228

Tourism Authority of Thailand (TAT), 274
Tourism industry, 1
Tourism Satellite Accounting, 22
Tourism services, liberalization of, 141
Traditional beliefs, commoditization of, 136
Traditional source markets, 4
Travel Activities and Motivation Survey (TAMS), 247

Uniglobe organization, 34
Uunionization, 133

Waste management, 32
World Tourism Organisation (WTO), 3
World Travel and Tourism Council (WTTC), 19